I08397AA

Then

Now

Thence

Make My Day – Book 32
Larry M. Henares, Jr.
Published, March 2018

Dr. Hilarion M. Henares Jr., known as **Larry Henares,** is a graduate of Ateneo de Manila, University of the Philippines, and the Massachusetts Institute of Technology, an engineer, economist, educator, big businessman, writer, civic leader, public servant, and hobbyist (guns, books, amateur radio and electronics).

He is a writer known for his essays on economics, history, art and culture, a front page columnist in the pre-martial law Manila Times and the most widely read column in the Philippines, according to all surveys, the daily "Make my Day" in the Philippine Daily Inquirer, after the EDSA revolt.

ooooo

Tatay Jobo Elizes, Self-Publisher

This book is published under permission of

DR. HILARION M. HENARES, JR.

This permission is subject to withdrawal any time so desired, in which case, **Tatay Jobo Elizes,** as self-publisher will cease publishing this book. LARRY HENARES is free to republish with other publishers. Tatay Jobo disclaims any responsibility for writings of the Author. Printing of this book is using the present day method of Print-on-Demand (POD) system, where prints will never run out of copies.

ISBN – 13: 978 - 1985891524
and ISBN – 10: 1985891522

No part of this book may be reproduced or copied in any form without written permission from Larry Henares, and Tatay Jobo Elizes. Contact; job_elizes@yahoo.com Websites: http:www.tinyurl.com/mj76ccq

ooooo

About the Book,
"THEN NOW THENCE"

Back to present times, Henares writes two letters to his 20th grandchild, Scarlet Snow Belo whom he will never see as a grown-up. He is 93 years old, she is 2, a difference of almost a century. He writes at the request of her biological father Hayden Kho who wants his daughter raised like the Henares children. In these two long letters, Henares tells Scarlet Snow of the heritage of mankind which is hers for the taking, of the Mother Principle which will govern her future, and of the career path she may pursue to be the "President of the World", as her father hopes her to be. The letters will be given to her when she reaches the age of 18, when she charts her own destiny.

For President Rodrigo A. Duterte, the first president of our independent country to disavow the colonial mentality towards Mommie Dearest America, which is the root cause of the economic and political devastation of our country, Henares suggests a course advocated by Don Claro M, Recto, of pursuing an independent foreign policy at arms-length equidistance between the two super powers, USA and China. He quotes Time Magazine articles that posits China's emergence as a mature power, leading the fight against Climate Change, building a new Silken Road infrastructure that dwarfs even the Marshall Plan for altruism and open-handed generosity, at a time when President Xi assumes power as a great leader, while the USA elects its weakest and worst president, Donald Trump, who eschews the imperative problem of Climate Change and retreats behind a policy of America First and racist bigotry. His essay on dealing and bargaining with China is classic, with a rationale based and the worst scenarios.

On Personalties, Henares writes of Kokoy and the Beatles, of the wonderful Alyssa Valdez, of Manny Pacquiao, of Muhammad Ali the Greatest of all, of Rene Knecht, of Rosanna his Perfect Child, of the biological mother of Opus Dei Father Bobby Latorre, of Cameron Forbes for whom Forbes Park was named, of Carlos P. Romulo, of Washington SyCip.

On the Human Condition, Henares narrates tales of UP and Tau Alpha Frat, of blasting nagging women to eternal silence, of Radio Amateurs, of King Arthur and the Witch, of the Mating Game, of a long lost cousin Nicole, of Spanish habits of eating too much and working too little, of the Fourth Age of Man, and why Jews are so talented and powerful, of War, of Florence Foster Jenkins who sung but could not sing, of Cristalle his grand-daughter's wedding, of Philippine Presidents, of Radical Islam.

Finally, Henares writes of our new President Rodrigo A. Duterte, for whom he drafted a Political Platform, speeches never delivered, a secret agenda never followed. He writes of his background as mayor of Davao City, admiringly as the first President ever to refuse to salivate the American *sphincter ani,* and liberally quotes articles of Ramon Tulfo and Teddyboy Locsin, who knew Duterte more intimately, and admire him greatly.

Henares reprints the entire Inaugural Speech of the President, and the "rousing start" of his administration in the days that followed. He takes exception to the observation that Duterte is the Donald Trump of the Philippines, the evidence being that Senator Bernie Sanders is more probably the Duterte of the United States. Henares writes of the Philippine presidential election of 2016, the candidates thereof, and why Duterte was overwhelmingly voted into the Presidency.

He now proposes for Duterte's consideration a proposal for a Federal Presidential Unicameral system of government, a unified Greater Manila government like Washington DC, and a "perfect" Constitution specifically forbidding family dynasties beyond the fourth degree of consanguinity, forbidding religious organizations from restricting the constitutional right to vote freely and the right to join labor unions for collective bargaining. He also proposes a plan of urban renewal by private initiative, without use of government resources.

oooooo

BOOK 32: THEN NOW THENCE
TABLE OF CONTENTS

oooooo

SCARLET SNOW

Part 1. Dearest darling Scarlet Snow,

This is your grandfather, Larry Henares Jr. If I were alive today, as you read this, you would call me *Laki,* which means grandfather in the province I came from, Pangasinan. I am writing to you at the request of your father, Hayden Kho, who wants me to help raise you even if I already will have passed away by the time you read this letter. I am already 93 years old and you are only 2 years of age at the time I write this. I am sure that I will not be around when you grow up to be a young lady, go to college, get married and have children. Once I made a speech at my granddaughter Angeli's wedding banquet and I will repeat parts of it in this letter to you, my darling, my advice to you in the style of the Spoken Word of Sarah Kay, poetic and to the point:

First of all, realize that you are part of a family. You were adopted by your mother, Vicki Belo, when she was still married to my son, Atom (A for Alfredo, Tom for Tomas, Atom BUM we call him) Henares, so you are technically my grandchild, part of the Henares-Lichauco-Maramba-Belo-Gonzalez-Kho clans. Embrace your cousins, aunts and uncles – they are your support group, your bulwark against a nasty cruel world out there.

My six children were schooled to love Shakespeare, and compete in national elocution and oratory contests; all of them won first or second prizes. I hope you will grow up appreciating Literature and Poetry, and if you are so gifted, Mathematics too. The advice I am about to give you will let you live in style, and as a person dedicated to Love, Truth, Beauty, and Goodness – like your parents and siblings. When you are old enough to recite a nursery rhyme, sing Twinkle Twinkle Little Star the way Larry Henares and William Shakespeare would have done it:

Twinkle, Twinkle, little star
Scintillate, Scintillate, globule vivific,
How I wonder what you are
Fain do I fathom thy nature specific,
Up above the world so high
Loftily poised in ether capacious,
Like a diamond in the sky

Strongly resembling a gem carbonaceous.
Twinkle, Twinkle little star
Scintillate, Scintillate, globule vivific,
How I wonder what you are
Fain do I fathom thy nature specific.

When you commit your first sin at 7 years, and pray to me in tears, I will from wherever I am, whisper to you gently: "Please remember, Scarlet Snow, nothing you can ever do, no matter how shameful, will ever make me love you less. If you ever get into trouble, never hesitate to tell me about it. I will never blame you, I will never say I told you so. And we will see together how to set it right and prevent it from happening again. My advice to you will echo in your conscience or in the words of your wise father."

When you fall in love at the age of 15, tell the lucky boy this:

Why do I think and think of you?
Why do you always haunt me so?
Why can't I ever find a place
Where thoughts of you can never go?

When you have your first kiss at 16, I advise you to recite this to him:

Before I heard the doctors tell the dangers of a kiss,
I really thought that kissing you was happiness and bliss.
Now I know biology, and I sit and sigh and moan!
Sixty million bacteria, and I thought we were alone.

When the time comes to make a friend, send a pot of soil with a plant and a bud, and a note saying, "Friendship is a bud, that withers in the coldness of indifference, but when nursed in the warmth of an understanding heart, blossoms into a flower!"

When you write your first love letter, or your first high school essay, I give you this wise advice:

In promulgating your esoteric cogitations, or articulating your superficial sentimentalities, beware of platitudinous ponderosity. Eschew all conglomerations of flatulent garrulity, jejune babblement, and asinine affectations.   Avoid all polysyllabic profundity, setaceous vacuity and grandiloquent vapidity –

In other words, write clearly, simply, sincerely, and above all AVOID USING BIG WORDS. For big words do not necessarily reflect grand thoughts. And it should be the presumptuous ambition of all of us, to be said of us, as it was once said of Winston Churchill:

"By saying simply and plainly what we feel, he has enabled us to feel it still more strongly; and by the power of his words, he has driven us to the limits of our potentialities, and has given us a vision of our own best possibilities."

And on your first lover's quarrel, tell him this:

Across the page of memory, your portrait looks at me.
I look at it and think again, of days that used to be.
A little smile, a little sigh, and then a tear or two --
Oh what I fool I must have been to think I fell for you!

And of course, if you want him to come back to you, call to him in this manner:

I call to you my darling, my voice echoes back on my heart.
I stretch my arms to you in longing, they fall to my side, empty, apart.
I whisper the sweet words you taught me, the words that only we have known,
Till the blank of the silent air is bitter, for I am alone.

When you get engaged to be married, tell the lucky man this:

I love you not only for what you are,
But for what I am when I am with you.
I love you because you are helping me
To make of the lumber of my life,
Not a tavern but a temple,
And out of the words of my every day,
Not a reproach but a song.
You have done it without a touch,
Without a word, without a sign.
You have done it by being yourself.
Perhaps, after all, that is what love means.

And on the first night of your honeymoon, tell the bridegroom this:

Do you not know why rabbits multiply?

Then darling, why not give it and try?
They say it thrills, it satisfies,
It brings to earth a paradise.
Birds do it and sigh, cats do it and cry,
Dogs do it and stick to it, so why not you and I?
Through all the years until the day we die,
Let's do it, darling, you and I.

The day you find out that men are pigs in their toilet habits, scattering their urine like a dog with a territorial imperative, have these sayings printed and hung in your comfort room. *"If you shake it more than twice, you are playing with it!"* And remind him that you are from Pangasinan, more parsimonious than the Ilocanos, teach him, to record every time he takes a leak with a counting system, four uprights for every slanting line, counting the times he pisses in sets of five, flushing the toilet only when the slanting line is drawn, to save on water of course, and to save on air too, because you have to hold your breath every time you piss. To remind him, print a poem and frame it near the counting sheet, *"If it's yellow, let it mellow, if it's brown, let it drown."* Then for God's sake, make sure he does NOT do it.

When you give birth to your first baby, recite this:
The birth of a baby, like the birth of a nation,
Is a mixture of pain and joy.
The pain rises sharply, till it is almost unbearable,
Then slowly fades away.
But the miracle of birth is such,
That when the pain passes, only the joy remains.

Remember that you are a Filipino, and as such you are a Big Fish in a Small Pond. If you migrate abroad, you will be a Small Fish in a Big Pond. But if you choose to migrate abroad, and/or if you ever feel like you are the Last Filipino among those who forget or denigrate their native land, plant your two feet on a plot of solid earth, fold your arms across your breast and say:

Wherever I stand, there lies the Philippines. If only one single solitary atom of matter exists, in a totality of nothingness that extends to the vastness of the infinite, then the universe exists, even if it only exists in only one single solitary atom of matter. And if only one candle flame burns, in a totality of darkness that embraces a universe of cold stars and dead planets, then the warmth of that candle flame can be felt, no matter how feeble, in the farthest reaches of all creation. And if the spirit of Filipino nationalism exists within me, even if it exists nowhere else in this benighted land, for as long as I live, the Filipino nation will never die."

And Scarlet Snow, if you ever have a friend who has loved and lost, or never loved at all, and comes to cry on your shoulders, embrace her and intone this poem:

The night has a thousand eyes,/ The day but one,
But the light of the bright world dies/ With the dying sun.
The mind has a thousand eyes,/ The heart but one,
But the light of a lifetime dies/ When love is gone.

My wife, your grandmother Cecilia, used to say, "To find riches is a beggar's dream, but to find love, that is the dream of kings." And I, your grandfather once wrote:

"To a middle-aged man like me, Youth is something left behind, as remote as the blush of the first kiss. But to my beautiful wife Cecilia, Youth is something that seems to have accompanied her all through life and never left her side. And I wonder what makes her forever young. And the answer is that she fell in love only once in her life, and never fell out of it.

"Lucky are they who loved but once and loved forever, for they never grow old, ever young as the first kiss. Lucky are they who like your aunt Elvira, your aunt Rosanna and sister Cristalle, can say on their wedding day, *'Two shall be born a whole world apart. One day out of darkness, they shall stand and read life's meaning in each other's eyes.'* Lucky are they who like your aunt Juno can say on their wedding day, *'Oh to be so in love that it would seem / No one has ever loved like this before / Or ever will...'*

"So, all of you who have loved and lost, or never loved at all, do not despair. Go and find the sunshine of love... to brighten your way through life, to light up your mind, and to warm your heart always. But if darkness falls upon you all alone, leaving you cold and lonely in the night of the last chance... Reach out for the hand that is offered, and walk out of the darkness into the light."

If you are ever called upon to make a toast, say this Irish toast that I composed:

May the golden sun crown your brow, and flowers bloom at your feet.

May good fortune dog your heels, and fair winds be ever at your back.

And may you stay in heaven for a long time,
Before the devil finds out you have been gone.

Finally, Scarlet Snow, ancient civilizations lasted thousands of years, while no modern empire lasted for more than 400 years. Why? Egypt, Rome, Greece and China had multiple gods in their pantheons, but no racial wars. Jews, Christians and Muslims worship the same God, but kill each other, sect against sect, and one against the others. Compassion, Tolerance and Goodwill usher us into what Thomas Mann calls the "Patriotism of Humanity", to underline the idea that human welfare is indivisible, and to demonstrate the greatest and the grandest Truth of our time --- the Truth of which poets sing and philosophers dream: That across all artificial borders of national sovereignties, above the diversity of political and economic systems, beyond all differences in race, culture, and creed --- lies, under God, the common humanity of man. It is this truth that makes men brothers. It is this truth that will set men free.

And when in the fullness of time, you take time out to fulfill your destiny, to do something spectacular to serve the human race, my darling Scarlet Snow, lift your eyes above the far horizon, lift them up to where faith and prayers and visions have wing-room, and build your castles in the air. Leave your castles in the air, then build foundations under them.

Plead, plan, plot and build,
Hammer, hack, hold, and build,
Yell, pull, push and build,
And build and build up to the stars
Till the universe shall know of your strength!
So that when all the stories have been told,
And all the songs have been sung,
And all there is to be has become,
Then you, the youth of today
Can turn to the children of tomorrow,
And to your parents and grandparents of yesterday,
And say, We have not lived in vain.

We have not lived in vain.

My darling Scarlet Snow, and whoever it is you choose to be your husband and partner for life, the Future is not in the Stars, nor is it in your Hopes, nor is it in your Dreams. The Future, my darlings, is in YOUR HANDS!!!

Your loving grandfather, Hilarion M. Henares Jr. *Wednesday, July 12, 2017*

Part 2. Scarlet Snow Belo's career path

This essay is addressed to my grand-daughter Scarlet Snow. She is the youngest of my 20 grandchildren, younger even than my two great-grandsons. At the writing, she is 2 years of age, and I am 93, a difference of almost a century. She is such a bright and talented baby, and to a grandfather, a baby is a source of high hopes and great expectations. I realize that by the dictates of an imperative and tyrannical Time, I am destined never to enjoy seeing her grow up and make something of herself. I am content to just write this essay for her to read when she grows up. DEAR SCARLET:

To begin with:

You have your free will, and will pursue your destiny in your own way, in your own time, so this essay will be in the manner of a suggestion and a guide. You father tells me that he thinks you should be a doctor who will manage the Belo Medical Group that your mother Vicki expects you to inherit, but he thinks you should go further and be the President of the World, hahaha! Don't laugh, it is achievable, and I will delineate for you a possible career path.

First of all, you have to develop a solid constituency to represent, on whom you can depend for support. Secondly, you must pursue an educational and career path that will lead you directly to your final objective. Thirdly, you have to be a genius in your own right, so people will look up to you as the best and the brightest, deserving to be the kind of leader you aspire to be. Fourthly and lastly, if you are to be a world leader, you have to have a worldview acceptable to the rest of the world, especially the poor nations of the world who are definitely in the majority in the United Nations Organization.

Constituency:

First of all, you have to develop a solid constituency to represent, on whom you can depend for support. Your 1.2 million subscribers on Facebook is a good start but such support may prove ephemeral. More dependable is your clan and family, the Henares-Maramba-Belo-Gonzales-Cancio-Kho relations. I know, I know, only your father shares your DNA, but the same is true of your mother Vicki Belo who has no Belo DNA either, only Gonzalez and Cancio. Family is more than just blood relationship, believe me. So embrace your siblings, aunts, uncles and cousins, they are your formidable support group in this cruel world.

Next are your schoolmates. Never make the mistake of enrolling in an international school where your classmates are children of diplomatic personnel, temporarily assigned to your country. International schools are expensive, but not will not give you a good education, or the desired roots in your society. You should realize that half of the education is making lifelong friends. In your high school, you will meet those with whom you will do business in the future, those with whom you will spend your social life; people whom you will have come to know, to depend on, and to trust; perhaps, even the special person whom you will marry and keep as a lifetime partner. Here you will meet your best friends and your worst enemies, your partners and business associates. Keep in touch with your classmates and schoolmates long after you graduate, they are the keys to your future. Go to a traditional school, where your mother studied, Assumption Convent, at least for grade school and high school, there will you develop lifelong friendships reinforced by a school spirit that transcends generations.

Finally, your countrymen. Avoid dual citizenships because that will dilute your love and loyalty to your country, and you do not want, when you enter public service, your constituency to doubt your allegiance to the nation. Stay in the Philippines, where you are a Big Fish in a Small Pond. Migrate elsewhere and you may find yourself a sardine lost in a vast ocean.

Education and Career Path:
Secondly, you must pursue an educational and career path that will lead you directly to your final objective.

For college, choose the traditional school your Papa Atom studied in, the Ateneo de Manila University where I studied. The reason I recommend it, is not that it is the best school. It is not, the University of the Philippines is by far the better school (at present about the 44th in all of Asia). Ateneo is classed together with de la Salle University where Papa Atom took his grade school and high school, and Sto. Tomas University where your mother Vicki and Papa Hayden studied medicine (about 175th to 177th in all of Asia).

The reason I recommend Ateneo for you, is that of all the schools, Ateneo is like Harvard; whole generations of grandfathers, fathers and sons study there. There is an Old-Money Old-Boy Network that transcends generations, you are not only connected to your classmates but also to alumni generations of the past and the future. Few Ateneans or Harvard men are ever jobless, there are always classmates rich enough to hire them. Ateneo is perfect for your pre-med course because the Jesuits give you a classic liberal education steeped in the common heritage of mankind: poetry, literature, history, fine arts, the performance arts, philosophy, in particular, Shakespeare.

We Ateneans love the Jesuits. Their classic liberal education give us what the Greeks call *arete*, a composite quality that has no equivalent word in English – "an all around excellence, completeness, wholeness in one's intellectual, physical, moral, and spiritual development. It denotes the man who has all the graces and refinements of cultured life, the man who can be eloquent in the forum, sensitive to a poem, clear and sharp with a pen, capable in business, courageous in the battlefield, superior in athletics. All this is more than a shallow versatility; it is the complete education of the whole man."

More than that, the Jesuits encouraged us in all our endeavors, "You are good, you are the best, go out there and conquer the world, we're right behind you!" A few years of that crap, and we Ateneans really believe it. You can almost smell an Atenean a mile away -- the swagger, the smugness, the air of superiority -- *talagang mayabang,* your grandfather, me -- now there is the quintessence of a pompous ass.

You should realize that your education does not end upon graduation. In a way, it is only beginning, for the field that you have chosen for your life's work, whether it be medicine, finance or accounting or marketing, is constantly evolving in new ways and new directions. To be educated is to learn how to learn by yourself. That is the real meaning of Education. So, dear Scarlet Snow, keep learning through books, through seminars, through interaction with your peers in professional organizations, be a student all the rest of your life.

For your specialty also choose Ateneo and the Medical City which offer a course which combines a Doctorate in Medicine (MD) and a Master in Business Administration (MBA) – perfect for managing the Belo Medical Group.

For your career path, choose to join the Presidential Cabinet and whet your reputation for Public Service, either as Secretary of Health or Secretary of Foreign Affairs advocating Medical Tourism. Afterwards be an Ambassador, preferably to the United Nations, where you can cultivate relationships that will elevate you to the level of world leadership. You may aspire to be the President of the UN Assembly, like Carlos P. Romulo, but this is only for a year and is largely honorific. Nobody except Romulo boasts about being one. If you want to have real power to change the world, aspire for the position of Secretary General of the UN Assembly, this lasts for years and is attained mostly by leaders of small nations.

The three levels of True Genius:

Thirdly, you have to be a genius in your own right, so people will look up to you as the best and the brightest, deserving to be the kind of leader you aspire to be.

You will find in the world outside that success will depend on certain qualities that you have developed in your school years. Often it is not brilliance of mind that will place you on top of the heap; you will find that the brightest in your class is often not the most successful. You must realize that there are really three levels of genius, and the best of this is not the one that gives you good grades.

First is the analytical genius; this is the pride of teachers and schools, the one with the highest grades and the uncanny ability to absorb and impart knowledge. They make the best teachers and professors.

The second is the creative genius who is the despair of teachers and schools, because like Albert Einstein, Thomas

Edison, Alexander Graham Bell, yes, even Steve Jobs, Bill Gates, Mark Zuckerberg and Leonardo da Vinci, they never seem to get good grades, are often school drop-outs, but are responsible for the innovations and inventions that change the world.

Third, and probably the most important, is the one considered street-smart, and not even classified as a genius. These are the ones never noticed by teachers and schools, those who organize dances, outings, elections, clubs and various extracurricular activities. And they are the most successful in life for they become kings, presidents and popes -- the not-so-bright who try harder to get ahead, the plodders, the ones who are dependable and trustworthy, who know how to get along with people and influence them to act towards a common goal, those with initiative, imagination and talent for organization and leadership. Above all, it is their Self Confidence that brings Success, a faith in oneself, a sense of destiny and pride that make possible the impossible. My daughter Rosanna, your aunt, when she was a little girl, wrote a poem that says just that. She wrote:

You are only as good as you think you are;
Swiftness and Strength can only bring you so far.
The race you run and the battle you plan ---
  You will only win if you think you can!

World View:

Fourthly and lastly if you are to be a world leader, you have to have a worldview acceptable to the rest of the world, especially the poor nations of the world who are definitely in the majority in the United Nations Organization.

Choose your advocacies wisely; breastfeeding, open borders for workers and refugees, climate change, above all, human rights, especially of women and the minorities of this earth.

Never forget that you are a woman, and that you belong to that part of the world that gave the world its first democratically elected female head of government, Madame Sirimavo Bandaranaike of Shri-Lanka. The Philippines had two women presidents before the USA had even one; more women justices of the Supreme Court than the USA has had.

A woman leader has a capacity for greatness rarely achieved by the male of the species. Firstly because unlike the male, she is motivated less by the quest for power than the mother instinct to embrace and protect the entire nation and the world.

Secondly, women have to try harder and accomplish more to get the same recognition that men get.

Thirdly, they are much more consummate politicians, used to persuasion rather than command, after a lifetime of cajoling dominant and philandering husbands; persuading and disciplining recalcitrant children; bargaining with vendors and peddlers; and making peace with intransigent mothers-in-law. They will have cultivated the supreme qualities of patience, understanding, and dissimulation to a degree unattainable by male politicians.

Fourthly, a woman is stronger in will and healthier in body than men are. Men can hardly cope with an 8-hour day, coming home to rest in the arms of a wife who never rests. The women has to be in better shape in order to withstand the pains of childbirth, the pangs of insecurity that is the lot of most wives, the 24-hour job of being wife and mother, weathering family crisis upon crisis without let-up. She has less nervous breakdowns and less debilitating diseases than her husband, and generally survives him. In the fires of life's tribulations, the woman becomes tempered steel, better equipped to cope with crises that beset a nation.

Above all, a woman has the quality needed to be a great leader and manager of the affairs of the nation, because she is a generalist instead of a specialist. Anyone who ever climbs up the corporate ladder to be CEO of the company, knows that the higher up one reaches, the less he practices the specialization for which he is trained. He must know about everybody's contribution to the company objective. He must be a bit of a lawyer, an engineer, an accountant, a human relations expert, in order to guide the varied specialists under his authority towards a common goal. The more responsibility he assumes, the less specialist and the more generalist he has to be. But all her life a woman is a Generalist rather than a Specialist.

To survive as a successful breadwinner, a man has to be a specialist, a lawyer, an engineer, a doctor; in short, a man has to be One Thing to everybody. On the other hand, a woman has to be Everything to somebody; she has to be a babysitter, teacher, guardian, policeman, warden, nurse, doctor, psychologist to her children; she has to be a bit of an engineer to be able to operate and fix household appliances; a bit of an accountant to plan the family finances; a bit of a lawyer to keep her family out of trouble; a bit of an artist to decorate the home; a bit of a wife and a prostitute, a bit of a chef and a courtesan to keep the interest of her husband. Even as she delegates her duties to her children and servants, she becomes to all intents and purposes, General Manager of the home. As such, she acquires the empathy, experience and judgment invaluable in exercising the leadership of a nation.

Small wonder then that when talented men attain a position of wisdom, prestige and power above ordinary men .... when they become popes, cardinals and priests, rabbis and mandarins ..... when they become Supreme Court justices and Kings ..... they are called upon to dignify their person with what women ordinarily wear .... a gown!

Women are much more valuable than men are. That is why we send men to war, and don't really care if many of them die, because they are dispensable. Imagine a world of all women and only one man. The world would not skip a beat, because in one ejaculation, that one man can eject 50 million sperms and repopulate an entire country; and his ability to sire children last up to 70 years of age. Imagine a world of all men, and only one woman. The world would be back to the days of Adam and Eve, because that one woman can only deliver one egg a month, and must wait out 9 months of pregnancy to have another baby, and her child-bearing years last only up to the age of 50.

The world is your oyster, Scarlet Snow. Read my book, Dawn of Great Civilizations, heralding the return of the Mother Principle, available at Amazon.com. I am giving you with this letter an issue of Time Magazine featuring "FIRSTS: Women who are changing the world."

You are young, Scarlet Snow, and I hope you have the courage to tell the nation and the world, what a young Ateneo student Raul Manglapus once said:

"I am Youth. I am he who dreams but who shall make your dreams come true. I am he who shall take the green of your pastures, the gold of your hills, the might of your rivers -- fashion them with my hands, my heart, my mind and transform them into life and power. I am he who shall take this nation which you will someday bequeath to me, breathe into it the warmth of my ideals, build it firm and strong and higher up to the stars till the universe shall know of its strength. I am he who shall think, work, act --- until the Filipino Tao, ill starred and striped no longer in the prison garb of self doubt and colonial double allegiance, shall stand head high in pride and dignity on every field and valley of this land. I am a laborer, I am a builder, I am a dreamer. I am Youth! Heed me, for the future is mine!"

October 2, 2017

ooooo

DEALING WITH CHINA

Part 1. Dealing with China
Memorandum for President Rodrigo R. Duterte
        for President Fidel V. Ramos, Negotiator
From Hilarion M. Henares Jr.
Dated Wednesday, July 20, 2016
Re: Dealing with China

We are being railroaded into escalating the conflict with China. We could sue China for their assets in the USA and Canada but that won't work. We are being goaded into a situation without any real solution in sight. The President is his own man, let him consider the alternative.

Bilateral Negotiations with China may prove to be a win-win proposition for both the Philippines and China, if we proceed on the basis that China will always be our neighbor in this part of the world, and that we must avoid being cannon fodder in the quarrels of strong nations, and negotiate for:

1. Kicking the problem down the road 50 years hence, not pressing our individual claims for the next 50 years and maintaining a status quo in the disputed areas, after which we shall renegotiate, taking account of such external factors as the geopolitical rivalry between powerful nations and the future actions of other claimant nations – with the Philippines taking a non-aligned position to avoid being "a mouse trampled upon in the battle between elephants";

2. During which time, the disputed areas will be jointly developed for its resources on a 50-50% basis, the treaty parties enjoying shared fishing rights, joint responsibility for environmental protection, shared use of manufactured islands, and "most favored nation" relations between the two countries -- with any dispute to be submitted to the International Court of Justice for resolution;

3. During which time, the Chinese government provides the Philippines soft development loans at 1% annual interest, for a Digital Highway for our Internet, and a Railway System throughout the Philippines including inter-island bridges and ferries, and for other infrastructures, with only the loan interests payable during the 50-year period;

4. During such period, the Philippines will never consent to being admitted as a State of the United States of America, since historically both the Philippines and the United States have unequivocally rejected such possibility.

5. The signed Treaty will be ratified according to each other's Constitutions.

Rationale, based on worst case scenarios:

To deal with China, one must consider Chinese historical experience with the Western powers (1841-1900), led by Great Britain assisted by Americans, Japanese and other Europeans, which systematically poisoned their people with opium, violated their sovereignty with gunboat diplomacy, treated their culture and pride as the oldest surviving civilization, with undisguised contempt, and surrounded them with military bases (1945-present), in Japan, Philippines and Taiwan. We also must consider that never in their history did the Chinese ever succeeded in colonizing any other nation; they were conquered several times by Kublai Khan among others but managed to civilize and absorb them into their culture; that they deliberately destroyed Zeng He's fleet, the greatest naval fleet of all time (1405-1445), because they found it unnecessary and undesirable to intimidate or conquer other peoples.

Part of the reason the Chinese are so aggressive in the Spratleys, is the presence of the US Fleet in the Philippines via the VFA and EDCA Agreements, putting them within striking distance of intercontinental missiles and nuclear warheads. Rightly or wrongly, the Chinese suspect that war is inevitable because the American military-industrial complex has a vast array of weapons fast getting useless and obsolete; because China is acquiring many assets in the USA, and will soon overtake the GDP of the USA by 2026; because the USA has trillions of dollars owed to the Chinese, which is almost impossible to pay back and which gives the Chinese the increasing ability to decimate the American economy; because the only viable way to maintain American superiority is to go to war soon, confiscate all Chinese assets in the USA, and renounce all dollar obligations to China. The Chinese feel that under a Republican Administration, which went to war with Iraq under false and invented assumptions that it had "weapons of mass destruction" and complicity in the attack on the Twin

Towers, and which went to war to occupy the Philippines "to civilize and Christianize" a people who were already civilized and Christian – the USA may indeed go to war with China for reasons of its own. If or when this happens, the Philippines will be the first victim of the nuclear war.

Quod Erat Demonstrandum.

Rationale, based on the best case scenarios:

For centuries white men imposed their brand of Western colonialism with the cross and the sword, causing untold suffering on the rest of the human race. For centuries long before that, the Chinese have practiced their own brand of Colonialism. They came not to conquer, but to trade. They came not to govern, but to spin their silken threads of credit to monopolize trade, to bind by debt, as completely as ever a serf was bound to land, virtually unnoticed, in wholesaling, retailing and banking, the economic circulatory system of any body politic. The last thing the Chinese want is control of a foreign government; governing is a liability; the assets are in profitable trade. Who wants to assume the cares and costs of maintaining the police and the fire departments, and collecting the taxes of a city, if he could operate its profitable department stores? The Chinese overseas traders have realized this for untold centuries. Unobtrusive, low profiled, it is they who have been the great imperialists, eschewing glory, even accepting insult, sticking only to business, willing to pay the cost of government, in short, to corrupt it, without hypocrisy, knowing that it is impossible to do business without it. They will never go to war to conquer us, it is easier to profit from our business.

For most Filipinos, including Filipino-Americans in the USA and those with Dual Citizenships, the Americans are generous elder brothers who gave us democracy, universal education, potable water and junk food, who will die for us as much as we are willing to die for them in Vietnam, Korea and against Communists and Muslim terrorists. Let us not delude ourselves, the USA never offered to defend us against **our** enemies, against the British and the Australians when they mobilized for a preemptive strike against us when we claimed Sabah from the British North Borneo Co.; against the Malaysians when they were supplying modern arms to our Muslim dissidents. The only time the USA will defend us is if we become

its 51st State. As for that possibility, let us forget it. When at the start of the 20th century, Felipe Buencamino the Elder and Trinidad Pardo de Tavera went to the Washington to consult Secretary of War and subsequently Secretary of State Elihu Root on statehood, he said: "We already have 1 million niggers in this country, why should we admit 8 million more niggers?" And doused the hopes of these two mestizo *Federalista* leaders who thought they were whites. Will the USA add 100 million Filipinos to its 325 million citizens, giving us 124 congressmen, and 10 senators if we exercise the "Texas Option" to split into 5 states? making us the biggest political constituency in the USA, with enough political clout to elect Jojo Binay as the American president? Will the racist Republicans allow it? *Ruat Coelum!* the heavens will fall!
July 20, 2016

Part 2. Bargaining with China
Memorandum to President Fidel V. Ramos, negotiator
From Hilarion M. Henares Jr.
Dated Wednesday, August 3, 2016
Re: Bargaining with China
      In short, China installed a military base in Scarborough Shoal within our Exclusive Economic Zone (EEZ) ; the Permanent Court of Arbitration (PCA) in The Hague, on the basis of the UN Convention on the Law of the Seas (UNCLOS), disregarded the nine-dash line territorial claim of China, in effect, recognized Philippines' EEZ rights; China refused to abide with the ruling; bilateral talks are remote considering the initial bargaining posture of both China and Philippines with regard to the PCA ruling.
      As long as we plan to accept the support of the United States in confronting China on this issue, we would like to propose a plan to enhance Philippines' bargaining position as a countervailing measure against China's encroachment of our EEZ zone:

1. We should encourage other nations, especially Vietnam and Thailand to file their own cases before the PCA, knowing that to be consistent, the PCA will rule in their favor, and that puts added pressure on China to conform.

2. We should consider exploring the possibility of joint developmental agreements with the USA and other nations in the outermost boundaries of our EEZ. The United States should at least show some real support beyond mere words.

3. We should consider exploring the building of bases for fueling and stocking of inventories in the outer boundaries of our EEZ zone, for other nations such as USA, Japan, and European nations interested in patrolling the China Sea to ensure freedom of navigation. We may benefit economically by sourcing the fuel and supplies. And in case a nuclear confrontation arises, at least we are little farther away from the area of conflict.

4. We should eventually file cases against China in countries where it has assets to lose, like in the USA and Canada, for violating UNCLOS treaty on environmental protection, just as victims of Martial Law filed cases against Marcos assets in the USA.

5. Later, when we have the advantage, we should entice them to the negotiating table, either accepting their acceptance of the PCA ruling, and/or doing everything to get massive soft loans for a digital highway, and a railroad system all over the Philippines, including bridges and ferries between islands.

August 3, 2016

Part 3. China Pulling Ahead by Ian Bremer, Time Magazine

Five years ago, the consensus was that China, with its ballooning middle class, would need to undertake painful, liberalizing political reforms lest its state capitalist system eventually collapse. Today, it looks like China's political and economic system is better positioned for the future than those of its major Western rivals — as I argued in a longer essay for TIME this week. These five facts help explain why:

1. It has the world's most powerful leader

As last week's successful 19th Party Congress made clear, Chinese President Xi Jinping has no equals among the world's most powerful people. Xi spent his first five years consolidating domestic power, launching a wide-ranging anti-corruption campaign that swept up more than 1.4 million party members—boosting his credibility with the Chinese people while sidelining his political rivals. Xi's been so successful in the pursuit of domestic power that "Xi Thought", his personal political philosophy, has now been enshrined in China's constitution, making him the most influential modern Chinese leader since Mao Zedong. All this at a time when liberal democracies around the world are struggling to keep the ship steady. From the perspective of the West, it's bad luck that the U.S. has its weakest president at the same time that China has its strongest.

2. It reaps global benefits from a state-controlled economy

But China didn't need Xi's coronation last week to herald its arrival. While the U.S. economy remains <u>40% larger</u> than China's in terms of GDP, China's top-down control of its economy and state-owned enterprises means it can harness its economic power and channel it in ways Washington can only dream of.

China writes checks to befriend other countries, and it does so without the demands the U.S. typically requires of its loan-recipients (like adherence to human rights). Yes, the U.S. still has the almighty U.S. dollar, the world's global reserve currency, which ensures it remains a player in the global economy for years to come. But China has a proactive plan to realize its global economic ambitions—the jewel of which is the One Belt One Road infrastructure plan, a network of roads, ports, tracks, and pipelines that will tie together the economies of <u>more than 60 countries</u> across Asia, Africa and Europe.

China's state capitalism doesn't just power the country's economy, it gives Beijing the ability to strategically engage a fracturing world in a way that Washington, with its diffuse and independent economic centers, can't.

3. It keeps the population in line with state-created jobs...

That same top-down control of its economy and willingness to throw money at problems serves Beijing well on the domestic front, as well. Beijing has seen how tech and labor shocks have upended the politics of other major powers—it has no intention of following suit.

And make no mistake about it, the same labor and tech trends that have displaced millions of middle-class workers are now making their way to the developing world. But China's state-dominated economy allows China to ride out tough economic times with minimal risk of social instability by creating jobs that serve no market purpose. For years, Western analysts have bemoaned China's social-engineered stability as "inefficient", and they were mostly right. It just turns out that there are bigger problems confronting governments than labor inefficiency.

4.   It keeps the population in line by leveraging advances in technology

But China ensures political unity beyond just shielding its citizens' jobs from disruptive technologies; it uses those same disruptive technologies to better control its citizenry, and in ways Western governments can't. Beijing owns or dominates all the tech companies that will rule the future.

The result? In the West, companies use algorithms to expand profitability, making people better consumers; in China, companies use algorithms to make people better behaved citizens. And Beijing is doubling down—China is preparing to launch its "social credit system", which marshals a person's financial data, social connections, consumption habits and legal compliance to assess a person's "trustworthiness." That trustworthiness could then determine something as innocuous as who can reserve a hotel room without a deposit, to something as serious as deciding the quality of schooling a person's child will receive.

For Westerners, that has shades of Big Brother; for Chinese, it's a system to establish trust among citizens and deter criminal activity. Either way, it's an effective way of keeping disruptive social discontent at a minimum—or at least in check.

5. Others are following in its footsteps

The Chinese system can be brutal, inefficient and repressive at times, among other (valid) criticisms. But as the world continues to fragment, the Chinese governing model will continue to gain appeal, for other governments if not for their citizens. International demand remains for a successful governing model for developing markets across Asia and Africa, and at a time when the U.S. and European variants are looking increasingly dysfunctional.

Does all of this mean that China will "win" in the long run? Hardly. The world is fragmenting, and the days of a single colossus striding the globe and imposing its will on others is finished. And long-term challenges for Beijing remain—a Chinese credit bubble may be looming on the horizon, and China has the bad luck to be situated in one of the most geopolitically precarious neighborhoods.

But it's time we abandon the presumption that China's state capitalist model is bound to fall apart soon; increasingly, the burden of proof on staying power is on liberal democracy.

This is Larry Henares, making his comments on this article printed in the November 13 issue of Time Magazine:

Opus Dei economist Bernardo Villegas of CRC, board member of McDonald's Hamburgers, whose services have been associated with the American Center for Intelligence Agency, and whose Opus Dei is also the economic guru of dictators Augusto Pinochet of Argentina, Francisco Franco of Spain, Ferdinand Marcos' First Lady Imelda and brother-in-law Kokoy Romualdez – has been so consistently wrong about his prognostications that we economists validate our own judgments by citing his consistent errors.

He said that China is moving towards the US Capitalist System, but will ultimately fail as all Communist systems will fail. That is not true. The Communist economic system has allowed both the Soviet Union and China to industrialize, has given welfare benefits from cradle to the grave and achieve for them the status of a nuclear power. American Capitalism survived because it adopted the Socialist concepts of minimum wage and medicare. Soviet Soviet Communism failed because its bureaucracy could not adjust to private initiative and market forces. Chinese Communism survived and prospered because it adjusted to private initiative and market forces, and will soon overtake the US economy by 2029.

November 23-24, 2017, UNTV

Part 4. Advantage China, by Ian Bremer, Time Magazine

President Trump has plenty of work to do during his <u>10-day tour of Asia in November</u>. In Japan and South Korea, he must reassure nervous allies that an "America first" foreign policy does not mean the U.S. has ceded regional dominance to China. In Vietnam and the Philippines, he has to communicate deep U.S. interest in balancing China's influence in Southeast Asia.

But the most important stop will be in Beijing, where Trump will meet President Xi Jinping for the first time since the Chinese leader heralded a "new era" in global politics at his pivotal party congress in October. Trump will try to project strength while calling for closer cooperation on North Korea and on resolving trade disputes. But he arrives at a moment when China, not the U.S., is the single most powerful actor in the global economy.

The Chinese authoritarian-capitalist model wasn't supposed to survive in a global free market, let alone thrive. As recently as five years ago, there was consensus that China would one day need fundamental political reform for the state to maintain its legitimacy and that China could not sustain its state capitalist system. Today China's political and economic system is better equipped and perhaps even more sustainable than the American model, which has dominated the international system since the end of World War II. While the U.S. economy remains the world's largest, China's ability to use state-owned companies to boost the party's domestic and foreign influence ensures that the emerging giant is on track to surpass U.S. GDP in 2029, according to the Center for Economics and Business Research.

The U.S. is hardly irrelevant. The dollar remains the global reserve currency, an exorbitant privilege that will likely last for years to come. Wealthy Chinese continue to invest in U.S. real estate and send their kids to U.S. schools. But the pillars of U.S. power—its military alliances, its trade leadership and its willingness to promote Western political values—are eroding.

At the same time, the leaders of other emerging powers—not just Russia but also democracies like India and Turkey—are following China's lead in building systems where government embraces commerce while tightening control over domestic politics, economic competition and control of information. This process has been in motion for many years, but China now has its strongest leader in decades, and the U.S. has its weakest. Americans and Europeans have always assumed that the long arc of human development bends toward liberal democracy. What if they're wrong?

There's an old, likely apocryphal story that, during a visit to China several decades ago, economist and free-market fundamentalist Milton Friedman visited a site where workers were building a canal. When he asked his host why the workers were using shovels and wheelbarrows rather than modern equipment like tractors, he was told that the project's purpose was to create jobs. If it's jobs you want, Friedman asked, why not give the workers spoons instead of shovels?

Times have changed since then, but not all that much—the reality remains that it is far easier for Xi to command Chinese officials to create and protect jobs than, for example, it was for Barack Obama to persuade Republican lawmakers to bail out the U.S. auto industry in the wake of the U.S. financial crisis.

China is announcing its intention to lead the world by building almost everywhere on it. Beijing offers direct financial and political support for its strategic industries, 365 days a year. The government protects Chinese companies charged with stealing the intellectual property of foreign firms. It provides direct funding for strategic sectors. It writes laws designed specifically to help them grow. And it engages in industrial espionage and cyberattacks against foreign competitors.

This level of protection is especially important in an age when the most important variables globally will be the pace and scale of technological change. Automation has already upended labor demographics in the developed world; 87.8% of manufacturing jobs lost in the U.S. between 2000 and 2010 were the result of automation and improved technology, according to a 2015 study by Ball State University. Technological upheaval is now poised to displace hundreds of millions of workers in the developing world, including many who have only recently risen from poverty. But the Chinese government's finer control of its economy will help absorb some of the shock that will have bigger effects elsewhere.

Take China's big three oil companies. CNOOC, PetroChina and Sinopec have each benefitted from large infusions of cash from the state via state-owned banks.

Similarly, the heavily indebted state-owned chemical giant ChemChina was able to acquire Swiss firm Syngenta and its biotech assets for $43 billion only because the Chinese government made clear that food security in China is a strategic priority—and that the state would guarantee ChemChina's financial stability. Private firms benefit too. Telecoms firm Huawei is poised to dominate the global deployment of fifth-generation mobile infrastructure, particularly in developing countries, thanks to a hefty credit line from China Development Bank, which lends in support of the Chinese government's policy agenda. Trump can only envy the Chinese government's ability to use policy and subsidy to decide which companies will win and which will lose—and the power that that reflects on the ruling party.

But jobs and industry are not the only ways that China's leaders ensure political unity. They also use technology to bolster the ruling party's political control in ways that Western governments can't. As we embark on the world's biggest social experiment ever—entire generations interacting with society primarily through smartphones—we'll see enormous power for institutions that have the means to control those interactions and the data they produce.

In the West, companies use algorithms to expand profitability, while citizens use them to become better-informed consumers. In China, companies use algorithms at the behest of the government to ensure that citizens remain within the rules of order set by the political leadership. There is no better example of this than the "social credit system" that China is developing, a system that allows state officials to assess a person's financial data, social connections, consumption habits and respect for the law to establish the citizen's "trustworthiness."

Imagine a credit report that reveals whether you've ever committed a crime, been caught cheating on a test, been drunk in public, missed an alimony payment, been fired from a job, signed a petition, visited undesirable websites, been photographed at a protest or written something on the Internet that led administrators to question your loyalty to the state. A good social credit score could lead to a promotion, a raise, a better apartment, admission to a good school, access to state-approved dating websites, better stores, better doctors, the right to travel, a more generous pension and important opportunities for your children. A bad score could put you in jail.

The potential for intrusion into 1.4 billion personal lives is unprecedented. Published information on the plan by China's State Council says it is intended as a safeguard against, among other things, "conduct that seriously undermines ... the normal social order" and "assembling to disrupt social order [and] endangering national defense interests." The plan's ultimate purpose, according to Chinese officials, is to "allow the trustworthy to roam everywhere under heaven while making it hard for the discredited to take a single step." For Westerners, this is a shocking abuse of state power and an unthinkable invasion of personal privacy. In China, these are the tools officials will use to build a more "harmonious society." China's largest dating site, Baihe, already allows users to display their credit scores in their dating profiles.

But China's most important ambitions are in artificial intelligence. This is the space race of the 21st century, but one with a much more direct impact on the lives and livelihoods of citizens. The biggest technological breakthroughs in AI will demand the kind of planning and investment that the U.S. once poured into the Manhattan Project or the race to the moon. However, the U.S. government no longer has the political will to muster this kind of sustained long-term commitment and has outsourced innovation to Silicon Valley. U.S. tech firms will have the advantage if the race to develop AI depends mainly on experimentation and innovation in multiple areas at once. But China is the better bet to win if the decisive factor is depth of commitment to a single goal and the depth of pockets in pursuing it. The one certainty here is that Washington—and the representative democracy and free-market capitalism it champions—is not in the race.

To argue that China's system is better able to withstand the shocks of today's world is not to claim that it's better for those who live within it. Political repression and the lack of rule of law in China create injustice at every level of society.

As local governments and companies in China struggle with debt, the state's ability to bail them out is not inexhaustible. Despite its investments in new technologies, automation and machine learning will displace large numbers of Chinese workers over time, creating long-term risks of social unrest. But for the foreseeable future, China is likely to remain strong and stable. Its international presence will continue to grow, and it is not short of ambition. In October, Xi said it was time for China to "take center stage in the world."

The China striding into that spotlight is not guaranteed to win the future. In this fragmenting world, no one government will have the international influence required to continue to set the political and economic rules that govern the global system. But if you had to bet on one country that is best positioned today to extend its influence with partners and rivals alike, you wouldn't be wise to back the U.S. The smart money would probably be on China.
November 20-22, 2017, UNTV

Part 5. China's New Silk Road, by Charlie Campbell, Time Magazine

On China's remote western frontier with Kazakhstan, yurts and camels are silhouetted against a piercing blue sky. Yet the most striking image rising from the desert is an entirely new city. Founded four years ago, Khorgos is poised to become the world's busiest inland port, a vital link in China's multi-billion dollar plan to <u>re-create the Silk Road</u>.

Some $8 billion of trade passes through each year, say Chinese officials. There's a free-trade zone that welcomes 30,000 traders daily, and an industrial complex of factories where manufacturers enjoy perks such as two years of free rent courtesy of the Chinese government. At the customs gate, trucks line up stacked with agricultural equipment and huge cross sections of blue industrial piping, as blurry-eyed drivers chain-smoke out of their cab windows.

"Today, the ground of Khorgos is mud," says Guo Jianbin, deputy director of the Khorgos Economic Development Zone administration committee, accenting his words with a booted stamp. "But soon it will be paved with gold."

Khorgos is a linchpin in Chinese President Xi Jinping's signature Belt and Road Initiative. Formerly known as One Belt One Road, it's a rekindling of the ancient Silk Road through a staggeringly ambitious plan to build a network of highways, railways and pipelines linking Asia via the Middle East to Europe and south through Africa. The economic land "belt" takes cargo, in large part via Khorgos, through Eurasia. A maritime "road" links coastal Chinese cities via a series of ports to Africa and the Mediterranean. A total of 900 separate projects have been earmarked at a cost of $900 billion, according to the China Development Bank. There's the $480 million Lamu deep-sea port in Kenya, which will eventually be connected via road, railway and pipeline to landlocked South Sudan and Ethiopia and right across Africa to Cameroon's port of Douala. A new $7.3 billion pipeline from Turkmenistan will bring China an extra 15 billion cubic meters of gas annually. Not since the hordes of Genghis Khan galloped west in the 13th century have such sweeping transnational ambitions emanated from China, though instead of ashes and sun-bleached bones, this time the invaders plan to leave harbors, pipelines and high-speed rail in its wake.

"Exchange will replace estrangement, mutual learning will replace clashes, and coexistence will replace a sense of superiority," Xi told the opening of the Belt and Road Forum in Beijing in May.

It's a vision of inclusive globalization that bolsters Chinese leadership credentials at a time when the U.S. is wavering on its international commitments. Belt and Road spans some 65 countries, covering 70% of the planet's population, three-quarters of its energy resources, a quarter of goods and services and 28% of global GDP—some $21 trillion. Beijing's rationale is clear: these are large, resource-rich nations within its reach, with a severe infrastructure deficit, which China has the resources and expertise to correct. By boosting connectivity, China can spur growth in the short term, gain access to valuable natural resources in the mid term and create new booming markets for its goods long into the future.

In March, China's Commerce Minister Zhong Shan said Chinese firms had already contributed 180,000 jobs and nearly $1.1 billion in tax revenue along the Belt and Road. Increasing numbers of Chinese engineers, crane operators and steel smelters stand to reap the benefits of maturing projects.

"You'll have a China that really sits at the beating heart strategically and economically of this most important part of the world," says professor Nick Bisley, an Asia expert at Australia's La Trobe University.

For Xi, that's the rightful position of the world's most populous nation, boasting its second-biggest economy after that of the U.S. China's recent history has lurched from colonization to devastating war and then collectivized economic turmoil, poverty and political strife. No longer. Today, Chinese companies own storied European soccer teams, a major Hollywood film studio and New York's Waldorf Astoria hotel. China has the most solar panels, wind turbines, and high-speed rail in the world. When, in January, Xi became the first Chinese leader to address the World Economic Forum in Davos, he presented an image of a confident, globalist, responsible statesman, helping to set international rules of trade and environmental standards.

This vision contrasts starkly with U.S. President Donald Trump, who can't pass his own $1 trillion plan to rebuild the nation's crumbling roads, bridges and electricity grid, despite the vast majority of Americans recognizing the urgent need. Trump's nixing of American involvement in the Trans-Pacific Partnership trade agreement, and open questioning of key Asian alliances, have weakened the U.S. as a Pacific power. Trump's stalled attempts to renegotiate NAFTA have irked neighbors Canada and Mexico, while his announcement of America's withdrawal from the Paris climate accord has left the world looking to China for leadership on this and other issues.

Restoring the lost grandeur of the Silk Road has myriad challenges, of course, chiefly the questionable economics of pouring millions of dollars into some of the world's poorest and most unstable nations. Falling commodity prices have undermined some projects, while others are vulnerable to crises or shifting political winds in host countries.

The scale of the challenge is evident in Khorgos, through which trains now chug on a 7,000-mile journey from 27 Chinese manufacturing hubs to 11 cities in Europe. It's the world's longest international freight line, broadly following the path of the old Silk Road caravans that lugged pistachios, ivory and dates to eager markets in the West. Guo says 2,050 cargo trains passed by Khorgos last year, and the goal for 2017 is 5,000.

Khorgos sits on the edge of the Taklamakan Desert, nicknamed the "Sea of Death." Herodotus wrote in his *Histories* of griffins guarding golden treasure at the desert's craggy northern extreme, and of the North Wind gushing from a mountain cave here. Lying just 100 miles from the Eurasian pole of inaccessibility—the farthest point on earth from any ocean—Khorgos remains one of the most remote spots on earth

Today, the Taklamakan fills part of China's westernmost autonomous region of Xinjiang, which borders seven Central and South Asian nations and is thus the central hub for Belt and Road's land portion. A total of 3,500 miles of the ancient Silk Road passes through this Alaska-sized territory, where the Taklamakan's dunes to the south are separated from a lush northern prairie by a central spine of meringue-peaked mountains.

But Xinjiang is also China's most volatile region, prone to <u>periodic convulsions</u> of strife from a predominantly ethnic Uighur Muslim population that feels marginalized and even persecuted under Beijing's rule. Riots in the provincial capital Urumqi in 2009 <u>left 197 dead</u>, according to official figures. Security is suffocating. To take a train at the Urumqi's railway station requires negotiating four ranks of X-ray machines and metal detectors. At the city's central bazaar, soldiers stand next to armored cars with bayonets affixed to assault rifles, as lambs are carried bleating and blinking past trays of mutton into butcher shops. It's China's only province without 4G cell-phone coverage—deliberately held back to impede the download of jihadi propaganda, say local officials.

In the especially restive south, Uighurs must secure official permission just to travel to neighboring villages. Many feel development isn't inclusive. "Things were better before," says a Uighur taxi driver in Khorgos, whose name TIME has withheld for his own security. "In the winter I would hunt wild turkey; in the summer I picked berries. We don't need all this."

Security is not just a domestic issue. Pipelines and dams in Myanmar, ports in Western Africa, hydro-electricity plants and copper mines in Afghanistan could all be held ransom to strife. Last year, Chinese railway workers in Kenya were attacked by locals who said the new arrivals had been unfairly prioritized for jobs. China may feel compelled to expand its military presence in trouble spots, shifting the global security architecture away from the U.S. In August, China opened its first overseas military base in Djibouti, and it now contributes more U.N. peacekeepers than the other four permanent Security Council members combined.

"Security is the most important challenge facing Belt and Road," says Zhu Feng, dean of the Institute of International Affairs at Nanjing University.

Economic questions also plague many aspects of the initiative. The ancient Silk Road faded in importance in the 1700s as more sophisticated ships began plying sea routes crammed with booty. Today, trains through Khorgos haul more than 80 standard shipping containers and stretching a half-mile long. But modern ships are powered by 110,000 horsepower engines and carry up to 20,000 containers.

The rail line via Khorgos to Europe is two to three times the cost of sea freight, with twice the carbon footprint, while only cutting transport times from eastern Chinese factories to Europe in half—18 days compared to 35 by sea. There are few goods that would benefit from this time-saving for the extra cost: perishable fruit or pharmaceuticals are flown by airplane to minimize spoilage; electronics or imperishable household wares are dispatched by the cheapest method possible to maximize profits. Compounding matters, while China sends clothes, electronics and building materials through Khorgos to the West, those same "cargo trains are coming back empty," says the official Guo. Europe isn't a cost-effective destination, and the economies of Central Asia are weak. At the Khorgos free-trade zone, only 10% of traders come from Kazakhstan. While the Chinese browse mink furs, Georgian red wine and Siberian honey, the Kazakhs queue for rust-bucket minibuses clutching plastic chairs, cheap bedding and counterfeit sneakers.

"Ninety-nine percent of our customers are Chinese," says Lian Gang, the manager of a duty-free shop in the trade zone.

The marine "road" faces its own impediments. China's ports had excess capacity of 50 million containers in 2013, according the think tank International Transport Forum, bigger than the combined volume handled by Japan, Russia, Taiwan and South Korea. But the current surge of new port construction, combined with slowing Chinese exports, means excess capacity will likely double by 2030.

Xi's personal patronage of Belt and Road means many questionable projects are getting the green light due to political expedience rather than economic need. A <u>new railway</u> through landlocked Laos, for one, is set to cost $7 billion—about half of the country's GDP. Some 70% is to be funded by Chinese investment with the rest paid for by the Laotian government, largely through loans provided by a consortium of Chinese state banks. The isolated nation of 7 million will never be a competitive manufacturing hub.

According to Erica Downs, a China specialist at nonprofit research and analysis organization CNA, who has spent four years researching the initiative, "If you can link whatever you are doing to Belt and Road, even if it's a tenuous connection, there's still a chance of securing financial support." State Chinese banks are obliged to support government initiatives with low-interest loans. Wary bankers have started referring to "One Belt One Trap."

When Xi first announced the initiative in Almaty in 2013, commodity prices were at historic highs. But they have now fallen precipitously. China is, of course, big enough to handle a few white elephants. Its meteoric rise over the last three decades was engineered on exactly this massive state-championed approach to financing, and it has the resources. Its GDP was $11.2 trillion last year, with growth at a slowing though healthy 6.7%, and a trade surplus of $48.5 billion in August 2017. In total, the Silk Road Fund—comprising injections Asian Infrastructure Investment Bank (AIIB), New Development Bank, China Development Bank, Export-Import

Bank of China and the nation's humanitarian aid coffers—adds up to $269 billion.

But the rest of the estimated $900 billion for the initiative must come via private Chinese banks and contributions by host countries. Beijing has enormous centralized power to get things done, including offering myriad incentives for business that embrace Belt and Road. Still, there is the danger that is has gone too far.

"The Chinese are very possibly taking on commitments that will exceed their ability to fund in a period of dramatically slowing growth," says Scott W. Harold, a China expert for RAND Corp.

Of course, it might not matter whether most projects offer substantial returns. Infrastructure is inherently a positive, regardless of whether its financiers handsomely recoup their investment. Roads, bridges and tunnels link communities and boost commerce. The Asian Development Bank says Asia needs $26 trillion of infrastructure through 2030, or $1.7 billion per year. Try telling rural Indonesians that a new power plant, which will let their children study into the night, is a bad idea. Or Sudanese farmers that the road or railway that will take their crops to market is an expensive folly. Many Belt and Road countries are so poor that even a tiny injection of capital can make a massive difference to livelihoods.

The China-Pakistan Economic Corridor is about befriending Pakistan so it stops extremists seeping over into Xinjiang.

Meanwhile, the AIIB, the new Beijing-headquartered multilateral development bank, was established in 2016 to fund Belt and Road projects but also to show the world that China can run a real, multilateral development bank according to international standards. Washington made fierce attempts to persuade nations not to join it, but few listened and 80 nations arenow members, including staunch U.S. allies Australia and Britain.

"When the Chinese government proposed the idea there was some misunderstanding, and some questions and even suspicions," AIIB president Jin Liqun tells TIME in his Beijing office. "Misunderstanding is understandable. It takes time for people to appreciate the concept."

America remains in denial about what Belt and Road really signifies. In a June report, the State Department commented that the Initiative's free-trade zones "only offer a degree of [liberalization] comparable to other opportunities in other parts of China" and not much else. The U.S. sent a low-level delegation to the May forum in Beijing. Chinese state media reported in June that Trump told a senior Beijing official he was open to cooperating on the initiative, though the White House wouldn't confirm those remarks. Then, on October 3, Defense Secretary Jim Mattis criticized the China-Pakistan Economic Corridor for passing through disputed Kashmir, parroting India's objections and appearing to side with New Delhi on the intractable territorial wrangle.

"In a globalized world, there are many belts and many roads, and no one nation should put itself into a position of dictating 'one belt, one road,'" Mattis told the Senate Armed Services Committee during a congressional hearing.

The new Silk Road is the purest illustration of Beijing's budding influence as Washington is consumed with partisan bickering and fumbles for a coherent foreign policy. China has wrapped an amorphous group of projects in a tidy package that speaks to inclusiveness, cooperation and altruism. It speaks of China, as an environmental leader, despite being the planet's worst polluter; as a champion of free trade and investment, despite wreathing its economy in protectionist red tape; as a good guy, despite acting as an authoritarian state that is a serial violator of human rights.

In Khorgos, this is no desert mirage, but a reality of steel and concrete, diesel fumes, and plastic sheeting.

"The next step is to diversify our capabilities: information, logistics, financial and an airport," says the official Guo. "And also tourism."

Big dreams for a small city that has its sights set on both East and West.

November 27-30, December 1, 2017, UNTV

ooooo

PERSONALITIES

Part 1. Kokoy And The Beatles

So George Harrison finally broke his silence, and gave a piece of his mind to President Marcos ("the old twit") for that incident when the Beatles visited the Philippines for the first and last time.   George recounted how the Beatles snubbed an invitation to Malacañang ("even in those days, we had taste"), and angered President Marcos who then "incited the island residents to kill the Beatles." He added that the Beatles were mobbed at the airport and were not allowed to leave until their manager gave back "the money we earned at the concert."

Georgie, that was only a small part of the story. You left out the best part, old twit.

When the Beatles arrived in the Philippines, good old John Lennon, the odd one who married the Japanese artist Ono, and bared his ass for the cover of his album, stated that he (Lennon) was more famous than Jesus Christ. Now, that was not a nice thing to say in Catholic Philippines. But the Filipinos largely ignored this remark because allowances have to be made for musical geniuses, even if they persist in being the Bad Boys of Liverpool.

As a matter of fact, President Marcos and the First Lady herself invited the famous Beatles to Malacañang Palace for a command performance before the cream of Manila's society including the Cronies and their executives, the members of the American Chamber of Commerce and the American Embassy, the peninsulares and the insulares. It was to be a glittering affair in honor of those who were more famous than Jesus Christ.

It was not a "mix-up" that prevented the Beatles from attending the Malacañang Affair.   It could not have been, because emissary after emissary was sent to the Rizal Memorial Stadium where the Beatles were performing, to inform the Fabulous Four that they were eagerly being awaited by no less than the First Lady, the President, and the pro-consul of the American Embassy.

The Beatles may have been disposed to amuse themselves with the President and First Lady of a banana republic, but having to pay obeisance to the American Ambassador is something else. You see the Beatles are British, and having been knighted by the Queen for contributing the most to the British foreign exchange reserves, they were understandably miffed at having to kowtow to Americans whom they consider former colonials and still uncivilized and provincial in their manners and morals.

So when the Palace emissaries persisted in taking them over to Malacañang, one of the Beatles show them the bottom line, "Tell those #%&*+><"#&%$ in Malacañang that if they want to see us perform, they better line up outside like the rest of our fans!"

It was a bright and sunny day, and joy filled the air with the sound of Beatle music, but there was no joy in the Palace, only the weeping and gnashing of teeth. And in the Overseas Press Club in the Admiral Building on the Boulevard, there was snickering and loud guffaws when Kokoy Romualdez (without his usual Mafia of Opus Dei led by Mario Camacho and Rex Drilon) and his two side-kicks J.V. Cruz and Maning Collantes came in for the usual game of Liars' Dice.

"Kokoy," commiserated Toto Olivera, "Gus Gonzalez, Larry Henares, Nap Rama and I are volunteering to replace the Beatles and sing for the First Lady. For the occasion, we composed a song, *'Torotot Na Naman'*, okay by you?"

Nestor Mata chimed in "Hey, Kokoy, I heard the Beatles will change their minds and play in Malacañang if you volunteer to be their mascot, you know, to replace Ringo's lost chihuahua."

Kokoy opened his mouth to say something, and Benjie Osias interrupted him with statement directed to J.V. Cruz, "Jayvee, do you mind telling your friend that the English language has certain rules? A sentence must have a subject and predicate, and no dangling participles, split infinitives nor double negatives. And for Christ's sake, tell him to spit out his words, not munch on them as if they were *champoy*. One of these days we will have to hang this guy for the deliberate and foul murder of the English language. No wonder the Beatles were mad, they are after all the compatriots of Shakespeare."

"Quiet, our master is thinking!" J.V. Cruz shouted, "I am ashamed of you guys. Our country has just been insulted by a bunch of fucking tonsils, and you make fun of Kokoy instead of organizing a lynch mob to teach these guys a lesson."

Kokoy was indeed thinking, because from his head issued something that sounded like gears shaking off rust and cobwebs. At the mention of the word "lynch", an electric bulb lighted up above his head, and Kokoy rushed out like Sir Galahad in search of the Holy Grail.

A few hours later, right on TV we watched the Beatles run the gauntlet of Kokoy's goons. A gauntlet is a practice invented in the Middle Ages, wherein two rows of men facing each other armed with weapons, strike at an individual made to run between them. A modern version was depicted in a movie "The Gauntlet" wherein Clint Eastwood drove a bus through a street lined with armed men.

Well, Kokoy had his version with the Beatles who were made to run a gauntlet from the airport to the tarmac at planeside, between goons who kicked, spat, punched, and elbowed them. Watching on TV, the boys at the MOPC sat aghast feeling awfully guilty for having mocked Kokoy into doing it.

When Kokoy swaggered in triumphantly, I stood up, shook his hand, and said, "Kokoy, you're an ordure in its most pristine liquid state."

"Thanks, Larry," Kokoy answered. And when Martial Law was declared, I thanked my lucky stars that Kokoy never learned how to use the dictionary. The old twit.
January 31, 1986

Part 2. The Rise and Fall of Alyssa Valdez

We quote Shakespeare. O Mighty Alyssa, dost thou lie so low? Are all thy conquests, glories, triumphs, spoils, shrunk to this little measure? Fare thee well.

The La Salle Lady Spikers have always been the better team, the best in the League, much taller, better coordinated, with a deeper bench, better than any team, past or present. Such stalwarts as Abby Maraño, Ara Galang, Kim Fajardo, Mika Reyes, Michele Gumabao, Cyd Demecillo, Mary Joy Baron, Kim Dy, individually and collectively, would have shone greatest in the volleyball scene, had they not lived in the shadow of Alyssa Valdez – just as brightly as Ben Johnson and Christopher Marlowe might have shone had they not lived in the time of William Shakespeare.

Who is Alyssa Valdez? Rewind back to the year 2013: La Salle had already 8 UAAP championships including two times 3-peat; became 4-peat Champions of the PVF National Inter-Collegiate Volleyball Tournament; became 3-peat Champions of the Shakey's V-league Conference; and heavily favored to win its 9th UAAP title with a 4-peat triumph in 2014. At that point, they were, to quote Shakespeare, "the choice and master spirits of this age." Then the miracle of Alyssa Valdez happened.

Alyssa led a 3rd-seeded Lady Eagle team without a single UAAP title, and had to win 5 do-or-die sudden-death matches on the road to the championship -- starting with first against 4th-seeded Adamson Lady Falcons; second, twice against 2nd-seeded National U Lady Bulldogs which had a twice-to-beat advantage; third, three times against defending champion La Salle Lady Spikers, with a thrice-to-beat advantage. The Ateneo Lady Eagles beat them all, one after the other, again and again and again, and completed one of the greatest upsets in league history by beating La Salle which swept all of their fourteen elimination round matches. They snapped La Salle's 30-game winning streak, ended La Salle's three-year reign as champions, and won Ateneo's first UAAP championship.

Who is Alyssa? She is the Lady Spikers' worst nightmare. Like Julius Caesar she came, she saw, she conquered. The Lady Spikers are admittedly the better team, the best in blocking, but Alyssa ran rings around them. She can strike from any direction, from the front, from the back, from both sides, making the ball travel like a guided missile, accurately into an unguarded space, towards any player with such stunning force that the ball spins totally out of control – and all the lovesick boys in the galleries, pining for this winsome lass with lateral dimples and a perpetual smile, wince at the thought of an explosive slap landing on their faces in payment for a stolen kiss.

How do you solve a problem like Alyssa? For three full years the Lady Spikers never knew how, even at the penultimate time when they were poised to dethrone the Eagles. At the awarding of the best players, three La Sallites received their honors, Baron as the best blocker, Fajardo as the best setter, and Macandili as best receiver and digger, while Alyssa Valdez stood alone as Ateneo's awardee, but she won more than all of them combined: her third consecutive MVP, best scorer and best server, P50,000 check, and in my opinion, with due respect to Jaja Santiago awarded best spiker, Alyssa is the far better spiker. Then later in the final Game Two, two sets down against the Lady Spikers, Ateneo won the next 3 sets in a 5-set game thriller. O Alyssa, thou art mighty yet!

But three days later on the 29th of April 2016, at Game 3, the very last day of the UAAP Season, the last day the graduating champions of both schools played together, Alyssa Valdez was at last vanquished! O pardon me, thou bleeding piece of earth that we are meek and gentle and proud. Live a thousand years, we shall never see the likes of you again, Alyssa. Hail, we salute you, Alyssa Valdez!
May 11, 2016, UNTV

Part 3. A World-class Asshole

I was inspired to write this, using a few words of Teddyboy Locsin, and embellishing it by adding many words of my own.

He was once a world-class boxer whose trademark was chivalry, making us proud of him! But beaten by Bradley, Marquez and the great Olympian, Floyd Mayweather, Manny Pacquiao became a world-class asshole by picking a fight with gays. Without anyone asking his opinion (who would?), he described same sex marriage as *mas masahol pa sa hayop,* in short, worse than animals.

"It is but common sense," went on Manny... but let me stop here, for Manny rarely finishes an English sentence, and besides, it is not common sense. What is common sense is Mayweather's advice to Manny, "If I were you, I'd fight only Mexicans, the pay-for-view is better."

But Manny persisted. In the only English sentence he ever successfully completed in his entire life, he asked: "Have you seen any three-way sex, sex change, hermaphrodites, transvestites, oral sex, homosexual rape or masturbation among creatures of the lower order?" Of course, he misspelled all the big words.

I got news for you, Manny. Plants, animals and insects are just as bad.

Imagine having to have sex without being able to move around. That is the problem with a plant who falls in love with another plant rooted one kilometer away. He solves the problem by enlisting the services of a third creature – bees, wasps, butterflies, even rats--- in a kind of three-way sex, or *ménage a trois.*

Sex change is found among *avocado* trees, whose flowers open as female in the morning and as male in the next afternoon, in an effort to avoid self-incest.

The *sea hare,* a large marine animal, has a penis just to the right of his mouth and a vagina in the center of its back, a real hermaphrodite. Just imagine what a wonderful merry-go-round sex orgy a group of sea hares can manage, getting their fun coming and going!

The transvestite male *scorpion fly* pretends to be a female, in order to grab the nuptial gifts of a rival male and present it to a female of his choice.

The female *cichlid,* a species of tropical fish, carries her eggs in her mouth to protect them from predators. The male has orange dots on his tail that look like the eggs, a tail he drags over the sand to trick the female into thinking she dropped some eggs. As she instinctively tries to scoop them up, she gets a mouthful of sperms that fertilize her real eggs. That is oral sex.

Homosexual rape is common among *anthocorid bugs* as a result of fierce competition among the males. The male rapist forces his sperms into the storage organ of another male while the victim is mating. When the latter copulates again, he passes on the attacker's sperms and genes.

Monkeys masturbate a lot, and so does my dog who licks his own asshole, and then licks my face. Yuck!

Why do I tell you this, Manny? Because by broadening our perspective on sex to include its biological roots in the rest of the living creatures, we may achieve sexual liberation. We can get the guilt-ridden ghosts from the closet, sweep up the tangled web of Freudian fantasies, and just simply have fun and enjoy sex. Why not, we may be the only animals who can!
July 21, 2016. UNTV

Part 4. The Greatest, from an Inquirer Editorial, comment by Henares

They buried Muhammad Ali on Friday June 10 in Louisville, Kentucky, where he was born and raised, after a Muslim prayer service on Thursday. Fittingly, people of all faiths were welcome to attend the prayer service for the man who, as his spokesman pointed out, "spoke of inclusiveness his entire life."

Inclusive, The Champ was. Also bad, brave and beautiful. Doggerel-spouting but sharp as a knife. That is to say incisive. Larger than life. Imperfect, contradictory, but brilliant in and out of the ring. Most of all crusading. Black and proud. A true voice for the voiceless.

"Another day at the office." Thus he proclaimed 40 years ago in announcing to ringsiders his arrival at the ring to fight the man he had called a gorilla. But it was no typical workday for The Champ, it turned out, for it consisted of 14 of the most vicious rounds ever fought in boxing. It was, a New York Daily News sportswriter would later report, every bit the promised "Thrilla in Manila."

If there was a fight that would define the life and times of Muhammad Ali, it would be this, the third and final encounter with Joe Frazier, described by many as the greatest heavyweight fight of all time. In 14 brutal rounds at the Araneta Coliseum, The Champ, arrogant and condescending, became all at once benevolent and compassionate, humbled and chastened by the unyielding stand of Smokin' Joe.

"Fighting Joe Frazier is like dying," he said in a post-fight interview. Frazier would not fight again and was bitter to the end, but it was the biggest compliment any prizefighter can receive from an opponent.

In 1967, the brash young fighter claimed conscientious-objector status and refused to be drafted to fight in America's war in Vietnam. "I ain't got no trouble with them Vietcong," he declared. "It ain't right. They never called me 'nigger.'" And he suffered for his principle: He was stripped of his title, fined $10,000, sentenced to prison, and forced to wait out prime years. He became the poster boy for the antiwar movement in the United States in the 1960s and 1970s, and was both hated and loved for his strong stand on racial, religious and political issues. He pushed the envelope, raised the bar, spoke up when it mattered (which makes, say, Tiger Woods seem like a wuss).

Said Cleveland Cavalier Channing Frye of Muhammad Ali: "He just gave June 10 the black community a lot of courage and changed our mindset: 'Hey, you can be a superstar and not be quiet. You can voice your opinion and be controversial and still be a champion.'"

After bequeathing the heavyweight mantle to the likes of Larry Holmes and a succession of lesser lights, and the money title to such diverse sports moneymakers as Woods, Michael Jordan and Floyd Mayweather, The Champ became a preacher of peace, spirituality and family values. And many were willing to gloss over his record of dalliances and indiscretions; to his adoring fans, he could do no wrong. His biographer Dave Kindred, as quoted by The New York Times, wrote: "We forgive Muhammad Ali his excesses because we see in him the child in us, and if he is foolish or cruel, if he is arrogant, if he is outrageously in love with his reflection, we forgive him because we no more can condemn a rainbow for dissolving into the dark. Rainbows are born of thunderstorms, and Muhammad Ali is both."

Who can forget him as, frail, slow and shaking, he struggled to accomplish the task at hand during the opening ceremonies of the 1996 Olympic Games in Atlanta, one of his last major public appearances? Millions all over the world held their breath and struggled with him as he persisted. After a few anxious moments, he managed to light the flame and send it creeping up to the Olympic cauldron that exploded into a spectacular ball of fire. Despite the ravages of Parkinson's disease, The Champ showed that he could still light up the world.

Muhammad Ali died on Friday June 3, 2016 in Phoenix, Arizona. He was 74 and ailing. The Louisville Lip is silent finally, but the flame he lit for the sports world and beyond -- for peace and international understanding and for racial, political and religious equality -- will endure. As will the world's memory of him, the images of him in his youth, in his prime, in his post-fight life: powerful, colorful, inimitable, the genuine article, for-all-time, quite simply The Greatest. End of Editorial.

This is Larry Henares adding his two cents to this tribute to the Greatest Fighter that ever lived, the greatest because not only did he win the Olympic medal at the age of 18; not only did he win the Heavyweight World title three times; not only that he won two of those titles against two undefeated champions Sonny Liston and George Foremen, both of whom who knocked out all contenders within 3 rounds, and fought him as 3-to-1 favorites –

as an underdog he shocked the world by predicting the rounds in which he beat them decisively -- but also because he fought his greatest fight against red-necks, white trash, and his own government that mandated him to join the war against North Vietnam, which he refused at the cost of his crown and millions of dollars of lost income. "No Vietnemese ever called me a nigger," he said. All state boxing commissions refused him the license to fight, his own government refused him a passport to go abroad for exhibitions. He converted to Islam and changed his name, and had to fight religious prejudice as well as racial prejudice. He fought them all and won in the Supreme Court.

I met him through Ronnie Nathaniel while he was in training for his fight in Thrilla in Manila in 1975. I was able to take picture of him as he was shouting "I am the Greatest!" and he gave me an autographed picture of himself. I was invited by George Araneta to sit at ringside, where I was splattered with blood from two gladiators who fought the most brutal fight in all history. Mohammed Ali wanted to quit in Round 13, saying "This is the closest I have ever felt to dying!" but his trainer pushed him to the center ring, saying "Your opponent is a lot worse." True enough, Frazier's trainer threw in the towel at the end of Round 14.

I remember the gala night in Malacañang after the fight. Everybody had a good time celebrating except the two men who fought. Mohammed Ali came to dinner, but could not eat because his mouth was so swollen, he could not open it, and the First Lady Imelda Romualdez Marcos had to spoon-feed him with soup. Joe Frazier could not make it to the party, he went straight to the hotel, where he went to bed hungry and sleepless with all his aches and pains.

I was also in pain when I learned of the death of Mohammend Ali, and I cried profusely that night, grateful that I was privileged to live throughout the life of this man. He is indeed THE GREATEST! Live a thousand years we shall not find his likes again!
June 23, 2016

Part 5. The Via Crucis of Citizen Rene Knecht
One would remember Rene Knecht, an old resident of Pasay, old in the sense that his family resided in Pasay for

generations, a bon vivant, who was a familiar sight escorting the richest and most beautiful girls of Manila sometime ago. He is tall, looks very much like a brother of John Kennedy and has been mistaken for one. And you know something, girls, he ain't married yet. He is tall, dark and handsome, he is rich, healthy and available. So sharpen your claws, girls, go to it, and good hunting.

Well, for a long time, we who commute between Makati and the Cultural Center, those of us who would rather pass Pasay and Cuneta than get stuck in Buendia traffic, have a bone to pick with Rene Knecht and his mother. It seems that Imelda Marcos, in one of her more lucid moments, decided to extend the Edsa avenue to the Roxas Boulevard through Pasay, which would in effect result in relief from the traffic jam at Cuneta Street. The most logical thing, according to Rene was to route the new access road through Cuneta Street.

But on Cuneta Street is the ancestral abode of Mayor Pablo Cuneta, the durable political leader of Pasay City, more popularly known as the father of movie actress Sharon Cuneta, and the beneficiary of a miraculous hair-growing compound, like me. Even more important, according to Rene, is that on Cuneta street are the various motels and places of assignation so dear to the hearts of politicians and the police. All these characters will have to move out and have their places razed to the ground, if the new access road passes through Cuneta Street. Well, Imelda reasoned out, there must be a better way to resolve this issue.

So the authorities decided to build the access road right through Fernando Rein Street instead. One also remembers Fernando Rein, which means oddly enough, Ferdinand the King. That was the place where the CIA had their safe house when they inveigled Secretary Jose Diokno and NBI chief Joe Lucban to conduct a raid on Harry Stonehill. With an IRS cover, the CIA boys occupied the old Arson building in the NBI compound, actually giving most of the orders for the Stonehill raid. But nationalist Diokno was uncomfortable having them around, and told them to go and powder their noses elsewhere. It was to Fernando Rein that they moved, with all the papers of Stonehill surreptitiously spirited out of the NBI compound, and copied on an old Xerox machine one by one. The local spooks, Colonel

Lee Telesco, MacArthur's wartime intelligence officer, and Colonel George Lizinski who lived at the Carmen Dewey Apartments would remember. They dropped in there to have coffee with Chandler and the boys.

Anyway, on Fernando Rein were the old ancestral homes of the oldest families of Pasay, among them the Knecht family. The old lady fought tooth and nail to keep her old house, took the case to the Supreme Court and won. So the work on the access road was stopped, the place taken over by squatters, Mrs. Knecht goes to the States as a permanent resident, and the commuters are still plagued with traffic jams in Cuneta Street. We told Rene that since his old lady has already moved out, and the place looks like Harlem, why not allow the government to continue building the access road and give some relief to the commuters. No, no, Rene said, the old lady's pride has been hurt, *amor propio na ito*, she will deny access to that road till the day she dies. And that's the bone we would like to pick with Rene. But we will desist, because Rene, like the Kennedys, is a mamma's boy, and will do exactly what mamma says. So there.

Damn, we almost forgot why we brought up Rene Knecht, the Kennedy of Manila's 400. Well, as fate would have it, Rene has a problem. And it stems from the very guys he and his mother have been fighting all these years -- the motel owners. And it has everything to do with Hotel Frederic, on Buendia Avenue near the Roxas Boulevard, which Rene acquired after the necessary endorsements from Tourism Secretary Aspiras, etcetera, on May 4, 1974, and which became partially operational by late June.

Now, the building was originally constructed by Manuel L. Dulay Enterprises, with three loans obtained from the GSIS from 1968 to 1973 with total releases of about P9 million. The last release was made in December 1973 and Dulay was subsequently advised that no more funding was available for him, and that he should dispose of the project. In the meantime, he was given a moratorium on interest and amortization till two years after initial operations.

By November 1974, upon certification from GSIS lawyer Manuel Lazaro Jr. that Dulay had P5.5 million arrears in amortizations, the building was sold at public auction with the GSIS as the highest bidder. In effect, his loan was current!

Rene Knecht consequently went to court represented by Rene Sarmiento of Quisumbing & Associates who recently performed with honor as one of the nationalistic Magnificent Twelve of the Constitutional Commission. Rene Knecht lost in the Court of First Instance, but obtained a permanent injunction from the Court of Appeals in 1975. In 1976, a compromise was arranged in the Supreme Court and the transfer of Dulay's loan to Knecht was approved. To this date this has not been implemented and in spite of the permanent injunction, the Philippine Tourism Authority has refused to register the project and finally, on April 9 1981, after Rene had two big NO signs in red lights hung on the Buendia side of the Frederic Hotel building, the Tourism Authority ordered the hotel closed allegedly on orders of President Marcos.

When Rene Knecht refused to comply without a court order, the building was closed by over 50 fully armed soldiers and policemen, who drove away the hotel guests. Rene subsequently tried to license the building as an Apartment building but this was not possible either, so Rene sought judicial relief before the 1983 Aquino assassination, after which he left for the United States where his mother was residing since 1980. Upon his return about April this year, he immediately set about trying to get the Frederic Hotel licensed, this being the logical thing to do. Sostenes L. Campilla Jr., Deputy Minister of Tourism for Tourist Services insisted on continued closure of the hotel.

Rene Knecht did not expect that the Motel syndicate that has been running Pasay for so long was still holding sway. The main stumbling block for Frederic is the real estate tax assessment from the City Assessor Luis V. Medina-Cue, totaling P19.5 million inclusive of the seventh floor of the building, since the previous mayor sued Rene to have demolished the top three floors for being allegedly unsound structurally after being constructed with steel frame by the AG&P.

By comparison, the assessment for Hyatt Regency Hotel, a much bigger and more plushy hotel located on the Roxas Boulevard, is only P12.5 million. The buildings were constructed two years apart. The Hyatt has about 4 times the floor area of Frederic, contains much more equipment, and is already operational.

Until the tax problem is resolved, Meralco will not connect the power lines to the building, making the building useless. In addition, Frederic is partially obstructed by an illegally constructed building between Buendia and Seventh Street. A second illegal building is now under construction further down Buendia with no set-back whatsoever and no parking place either, in complete violation of the building code.

To further complicate matters, the City Assessor Luis Medina-Cue has subdivided the compound belonging to Rene's mother, which is the subject of the Edsa extension case I already mentioned, and the City Treasurer refuses to accept payment of taxes unless his mother recognizes the subdivision as per the law passed by the defunct Batasan Pambansa. When Rene's administrator refused to pay on this basis, the property was auctioned without notice and the title thereto was transferred to SALEM Sales Investment Corporation. Obviously, Rene contends, the Motel Syndicate is still in complete control of things in Pasay.

As proof that the Motel Syndicate has control of Pasay, Rene says, another motel is presently under construction at the intersection of Fisher and Harrison through which Edsa is supposed to be built as per Supreme Court decision.

The City has also built a landfill bridge to the reclamation project in front of the San Juan de Dios Hospital without installing any culverts, thus blocking off the flow of floodwaters to the pumping station in Libertad. Whether or not this is part of the deliberate harassments related to the Edsa project, it certainly has caused the entire section to flood seven times in the last 7 months.

And that's the way the lay of the land goes.

That's what makes one wonder what is the use of fighting tyranny and oppression and injustice... when the dust of battle clears, the same kind of bastards are still running the government, pushing the ordinary citizen to the wall, driving him from pillar to post... and making him bear the burden of still more tyranny, oppression and injustice. How stale, flat and unprofitable seem to me all the uses of this world. Fie, fie on it, it is an unweeded garden grown to seed; things rank and gross in nature possess it merely, Hamlet would say. And he would be right. The new centurions of the Cory administration are not interested in correcting the injustices of the Marcos regime, they are interested in continuing the injustice and profiting from it. Bastards.

The Unicom and the CoCoBank used the coconut farmers' money to get control of San Miguel Corporation. It was an injustice committed against the original stockholders of San Miguel. You would expect Salonga and the PCGG to correct the injustice, and allow the liquidation of the shares purchased by Unicom and CoCobank, so that the San Miguel may be given back to the original stockholders. But no. The PCGG took advantage of the injustice, sequestered the shares involved and voted government people into plushy sinecures. Bastards.

Same thing with Oriental Petroleum. Imelda and Kokoy set up a corporation and maneuvered an exchange of stock with Oriental so they have enough shares to control and bleed it. The shares of their corporation have no value, the shares they got from Oriental was watered stock that diluted the value of the stocks in the hands of the legitimate stockholders. You would think the PCGG would re-exchange those swapped shares, cancel the watered stock and restore the value of the legitimate shares. But no. The PCGG takes over Kokoy's corporation and vote its shares of Oriental stock to put its favored friends into plush directorships. Bastards.

Same thing with the government financial institutions. Marcos' minions would drive the companies of their enemies to bankruptcy, with a lot of skullduggery and shenanigans, inefficiency and corruption, and the minions get replaced, but the injustices are not corrected, the same breed of vultures come in to feed upon the oppressed. Bastards.

Same thing with many of the OICs that replaced Marcos' *tutas*. They are as arrogant, lazy, inefficient, corrupt, cruel, unjust oppressors as their predecessors, whose web of criminal elements they just took over. Bastards.

Same thing with the military, the armpit of the nation. You would think they would deodorize themselves, clean out the murderers and fascists who crack the heads of civilians who could not fight back, the psychos who force coke bottles into vaginas and apply high voltage electrodes on testicles and nipples, and scoop the eyes with sharpened spoons or stab them with ice-picks, or pull out finger nails with pliers, and break kneecaps with hammers and baseball bats, or shove an electric cattle prod up the asshole, or drill teeth with a carpenter's electric drill without anesthesia. But no. These crazies and sadists are still around, insisting on protecting us from the communists, and shouting threats and obscenities at our nationalists, those who happen to love the Philippines more than they love America. Bastards.

In the next full moon, when witches and werewolves roam the labyrinths of blackness, when vampires lurk in shadows and ghosts haunt the dead of night, as the clock strikes twelve and Dracula rises from his coffin and bats at their belfrys, the corpses in their graves, gnomes at their burrows, warlocks and zombies and dreaded creatures take over the bowels of darkness --- take out your dolls, murmur incantations, stick pins into them, utter the curse of the undead, weave the devil's spell on these bastards, these leeches, these bloodsuckers in our government, and cast them out screaming in terror from the face of the earth.

Part 6. My Perfect Child

During the early years of our marriage, my wife Cecilia and I had five children, one after another: boy (Ronnie), boy (Atom), girl (Elvira), boy (Danby), girl (Juno). For years we were sending out Christmas cards, boasting of our, in poker parlance, Full House of Kings; Cecilia and I were the Jokers. For years we struggled to raise a family while I managed H. G. Henares & Sons, making Paints and School Supplies, including Mongol Pencils, Binney & Smith Crayolas, and Parker Quink Ink, and Cecilia was establishing her Henlich Mark (Henares-Lichauco-Marquez) factory of children's costumes and toys. Those were turbulent years of raising a family of children, most of them high strung, each of whom competed for our complete attention, and sent us scurrying to solve their problems, in school, in their love-life, in their *barkadas*, in their various preoccupations.

Then one day, six years after our 5th child, in 1965 when Cecilia was already 38 years of age, I was 41, and both of us were ready to coast along to a comfortable old age, an unexpected gift came in the form of a baby girl. Suddenly we are faced with the prospect of having to deal with another child to raise, at the time we are already in midlife crisis and starting to slow down.

She was born on April 22, a combination of our birthdates, my April and Cecilia's 22nd. We named her Rosario Anna, after Cecilia's grandma Rosario Roensch and Ana Yu Sycip (Washington's wife); and nicknamed her Rosanna, after Rossana Podesta, star of the movie "Helen of Troy".

Since the beginning we considered her our good luck charm and good fortune. She is the only one of our children who had a sitting President (Diosdado Macapagal) as godfather. She was the baby of the family, and grew up to be a perfect child. Never during her entire lifetime did this girl ever cause us any concern, not a single solitary suggestion or suspicion of anything remotely resembling a problem dogged her heels. She was absolutely competent, self-sufficient, independent, always in charge, and helpful to her parents above and beyond the call of duty.

In grade school, she augmented her allowance by going into business for herself, buying foodstuffs and selling them to her classmates at prices lower than what the student canteens were charging. One day, Cecilia was called to the office of the principal to face the complaints of the franchised stores; it was a day of great pride for her to discover that her little girl was beating the competition. "This is the land of free enterprise. I am proud of my daughter! Experienced businessmen should be ashamed to admit being beaten by a second-grade pupil!" she told the school authorities, and won Rosanna the right to continue in business.

Rosanna studied in the Assumption Convent up to second grade and continued in San Agustin College till she graduated from grade school; took her high school back in Assumption in San Lorenzo Village. Unknown to us and without getting our permission she fell into the company of male teen-agers all the way in La Salle Greenhills. Had we known we might have done a lot of investigating, vetting and getting her a trusted chaperone. We need not have worried. These teen-agers joined a theater group under Bro. Bernie Oca, and presented plays, all starring Rosanna in the female lead role in "Runaways", "Godspell" and "Grease". And she went on to join Repertory Philippines' staging of "Joseph and his Technicolor Dreamcoat", "The Best Little Whorehouse in Texas" among others.

Rosanna's advent converted our Full House of Kings to three boys and three girls, a perfect Balance Sheet. Our friends wondered who are the assets and who are the liabilities. And I answer: "A son is a son till he takes a wife; a daughter is a daughter for all of her life." My greatest pride comes with the memory of my three daughters going to Makati Med every weekend, as candy stripers, singing and dancing to entertain the patients in the Charity Ward.

Rosanna enrolled in UP for her Bachelor of Arts in Mass Communication. When she graduated, the first job she sought was teaching grade two class in San Agustin College. "Those priests in San Agustin were so good to me, I feel I have to teach there for two years to pay them back," she explained. Then after her first paycheck, she told her mother, "From here on, I will contribute to the expenses of the house by paying for the telephone." Later at the time she needed a car, she told her mother, "Just pay for the down payment, Mama, I will pay for the installments." Her mother cried tears of joy that night, saying, "No other child of ours ever offered to pay part of the house expenses, or to pay for the car she needed. Rosanna is our Perfect Child."

She was indeed our Perfect Child in every way. She was the favorite Godmother for all her nieces and nephews. She babysat for all of them. She never forgot their birthdays, and she always had gifts for them. She took them out to movies and to special events. "What a Perfect Aunt you are!" we exclaimed. And she would answer with mock sadness, "And who will take care of my own children?" And the sad answer to this question is "Nobody. When her time came, there was no other Perfect Aunt to care for her children, her sisters having their own children to raise and being too busy making a living."

She was perfect in many ways. She is the one child who never had to ask permission for doing what teenagers do, from buying clothes, to going on dates, to having a boyfriend. We had complete trust in her doing the right thing. Not only does she have this profound sense of gratitude that makes her pay back and pay forward for all things she received, but she also has this profound sense of rectitude that makes her do "the right thing", despite all obstacles or inconveniences. She always had friends, lifelong friends, who trusted her and accepted her leadership, and she saw to it that they behaved in the proper way, especially towards her brothers who are inveterate playboys.

One day, she was hailed down by traffic policemen for some traffic violation. She stopped her car and waited for the issuance of the traffic ticket while the policeman was telling her that she was liable for a P500 fine, hinting all the while that it would be more convenient for her to save time and money by settling out of court. She answered, "I am in the wrong, officer. Please give me the traffic ticket, I am willing to go to court and pay my fine." The policemen could not believe their ears, they probably thought Rosanna was a bit of an idiot, so they tried to explain their proposition many times. After practically half an hour of conferences among themselves and arguing with Rosanna, they finally and in exasperation let her go without issuing her a traffic ticket.

Another day, while she and her husband were parking their car beside their bank, Rosanna noticed another car already parked beside, engine running, windows closed and darkly shaded. Then one of the windows was slightly opened and a hand flipped a lighted cigarette outside. To Rosanna, this was a violation of the anti-littering ordinance. She knocked at the window insistently, and said, "Listen, you just threw a lighted cigarette on the sidewalk. I suggest you pick it up and put it in the trash can." She kept banging on the door, until the door opened. Inside the car, with engine running, were a group of men fully armed. Rosanna's husband Eric suddenly realized that this car was probably there to rob the bank. One passenger got out of the car, picked up the cigarette, and malevolently looking at Rosanna, brought the cigarette inside and closed the door, while several passersby looked on. Then the car moved in reverse and left. The employees in the bank never realized how closely they have avoided being robbed, because my Perfect Child just could not abide people littering.

I boast of reading one book every day from the age of ten to the age of 80, and of having written 36 books. Rosanna is the one child I have who inherited my love of reading books, writing essays, and making speeches. She won second place in the National Competition of the Voice of Democracy Oratorical Contest. She has a writing style full of sparkling wit and profound insights. And in the family she is the acknowledged master in the making of photo-albums, full of illustrations blending with appropriate comments, all arranged with an artist's eye.

Once when invited to speak before an audience of nurses, she saw many of them texting with their cell-phones, and she said, as somebody else would never do, "Please, you invited me here to speak. Please give me the courtesy of giving me your complete attention."

My wife Cecilia with a mother's concern, always had her say about her children's choice of spouse, except in the case of Rosanna. "That daughter of ours, our Perfect Child, will choose a perfect husband, you will see. A loving, loyal, faithful husband who will be tall, good-looking and romantic as I want him to be, and nationalistic, brilliant and financially responsible, as you want him to be." It was an untraditional love affair, played out according to Hoyle, no chaperones, the boy managing a unique proposal that involved a friend driving the Rosanna down the Boulevard, to see and read placards placed at intervals on the side walk, on which the message was written... WILL...YOU... MARRY... ME.... and there Eric Angeles was beside the last placard, with a bouquet of flowers and an engagement ring. I was ready to share expenses for the wedding, but I was told to back off, those two lovers took care of everything, including a vintage car to bring them to a San Sebastian Church uniquely made of steel, and a bride-and-groom official photo of the two joyfully dancing the jig.

It was not all joy in their years of marriage: repeated miscarriages, expensive treatments by a stateside Immunologist, the final birth of two sons, one by premature birth, the other needing therapy. For Rosanna it was a case of Challenge and Response.

The first was met with humor and charity. The first born was premature and had to be placed in an incubator. He was named Uno. And beside him in another incubator, was a baby girl named Isa. Get it? Uno, Isa and perhaps another named One (Juan). After a month of shared nursing (nursing each other's baby) with her older sister, feeling inadequacy of milk for her child, she called on all her friends who are nursing mothers to contribute their extra milk to her "Angel's Breastmilk Bank" (her married name is Angeles) which she maintains to this day as her charity work to help premature babies. Once she told one mother who did not want to breastfeed, and asked for breastmilk from her Bank, "I'm sorry, you are capable of breastfeeding your own baby. My Angel's Bank is free but only for premature babies whose mothers cannot supply enough milk." For this she was given awards by the Department of Health, placed in the list of "100 Amazing Filipinos" featured in the Reader's Digest and other local magazines.

Her second boy named Vigo, needed speech and physical therapy. She hired several Speech Therapists, but most of them migrated abroad where they are much in demand. So Rosanna decided to enroll in UP for the second time to get a Bachelor's degree in Speech Therapy. For four years at 46 years of age, she struggled with classmates and teachers half her age, and graduated *cum laude*, the first of her siblings to get such honor. Now, not only does she work with her own child Vigo, but she also finds time to use her new expertise as charity work for others in need. That's My Perfect Child.

Her husband, asked by a friend to join him in migrating to the USA, answered, "That's never been an option. I sink or swim with my country." And that's my Perfect Son-in-law.
January 20-22, 2016, UNTV

Part 7. My Son, Why Hast Thou Forsaken Me? written for Marina Donato Nermal

Dear Father Roberto Latorre of Opus Dei; I am Marina Donato Nermal, your biological mother.

I come from a family so poor, I was left in an orphanage for nuns to raise. After World War II, as a 17 year old lass from Pasi, Iloilo, I entered the service of Atty. Porfirio Dimayuga Latorre then the Tax Expert and a partner in the law firm Perkins, De Witt, Ponce-Enrile & Siguion-Reyna. Mrs. Generosa Almeda Latorre, who was known as Osang, hired me as the yaya of her baby boy Luis-Esteban, known as Teban, born August 25, 1949 at the University of Sto. Tomas Hospital and baptized Luis-Esteban Latorre at the nearby Sta. Teresita Parish; it is there where I developed my devotion to the Little Flower, St. Therese of the Child Jesus, who has guided me and my family ever since.

When Teban was one and a half, I fell in love with my future husband, Recaredo "Karing" Nermal, who was a male domestic and handyman/valet of Atty. Porfirio Latorre. Our romance bore fruit at the same time that Osang got pregnant with her second child. Unfortunately, she had a miscarriage, while I had a natural delivery at the government-owned Philippine General Hospital, or PGH.

I had a baby boy, born on September 26, 1951, and registered in the birth certificate provided by PGH hospital as JUSTINE LATORRE. I did not know this at first, since Osang took care of everything, paid for all expenses and arranged to have a fake birth certificate calling the baby Justine Latorre, child of Porfirio Latorre and Generosa Almeda. I trusted my employer Osang to do what's best for me and Karing, the father of my child Justine. She told me, "Kasi hindi pa kayo kasal sa Simbahan, nagka-anak ka na. Mabuti, kunin ko na lang ang bata. Mr. Latorre does not have to know! This will be our secret, babae sa babae! No one need ever know." Atty. Latorre was then traveling all the time.

That baby of mine is you, Father Bobby. I did not object to Osang's proposal, because she promised that I will be assigned as your yaya; that I and your father Karing will be well taken care of. I married your father who was given a permanent job at General Textile (Gentex) owned by the Yujuico family; Marietta Yujuico being one of the best friends of Osang. We were given a house on a 900-square meter lot in a prime subdivision in Binan, Laguna. I had three other children born at the PGH, as Justine was. And Osang paid for the education of all my children, in good expensive schools: Virgie studied at the Philippine Women's University (PWU) and later became a nun; Teresita took two courses, Chemistry and Nursing at the Far Eastern University (FEU) and at the University of Santo Tomas (UST) and is now in the USA managing a successful Nursing Home; and Jimmy became a board-certified Electrical Engineer after graduating from Feati University. You can see, we are NOT poor and engaged in blackmail as alleged by some suspicious lawyers. We want nothing from you, Father Roberto Latorre of the Opus Dei, who took the vow of poverty. This ad is paid for by my family because we are being prevented by some unscrupulous lawyers from contacting you and proving my claim as your mother through a DNA test. I have since left my DNA sample at the UP Center in Diliman Quezon City waiting for your matching specimen.

What happened to you, Father Latorre, my first-born? First, Osang immediately renamed you "Bobby" in honor of her husband's richest client, Roberto Benedicto, friend of Marcos. Second, I took care of you through all your childhood years, together with your Kuya Teban: both of you slept always by my side, and I embraced you as my son through all those nights. I loved you, Justine, and I agonized if ever I could tell you in the future how much I love you, when my promise to Osang expired, and you were old enough to understand. You followed the footsteps of your Kuya Teban, two years ahead, through La Salle, to UP, and on to Rome and Spain, as Opus Dei priests. You cannot imagine how hurt I was when you and your rich friends at the Opus Dei began to treat me as a lowly servant, whenever I came visiting several times a year.

Why am I telling the truth now? On November 14, 2009, Osang died; three months later Teban came to my house to ask why Bobby who was born in 1951, seemingly had no birth certificate; later Teban discovered a birth certificate with the name "Justine," but with an annotation in 2009, almost 60 years later, saying that Roberto and Justine were the same person; suddenly and mysteriously, valuable documents at the NSO began to disappear. I suddenly had to blurt out the truth because that was the right thing to do! "I thirst!" I thirst for the love and respect of my first-born, you Father Bobby/Justine Latorre/Nermal! You lose nothing, and as the Bible says, "The truth will set your free!" I am nailed to my cross? My son, my son, why have you forsaken me?
July 13, 2016

Part 8.   Cameron Forbes, after whom Forbes Park was named

William Cameron Forbes was the American Governor General from 1909 to 1913, under President William Howard Taft. He was a polo enthusiast who picked his Harvard staff on the basis of their ability to wield a good mallet and ride a horse. As a good Republican, he was strongly opposed to Filipino independence, presumably among other things, because the withdrawal of the US Treasury would leave him with no polo mounts, and no facilities to play his favorite sport. In his honor, the Ayala-Zobel clan named Forbes Park after him, and forever foisted the Manila Polo Club on us Filipinos.

My grandfather who was a revolutionary, a senator and a congressman before the war, used to tell me the history of the Philippines during the Spanish and early American Occupation. And he mentioned that Governor General Forbes was an idiot, but I did not believe me, because he regarded all Americans in the Philippines as Neanderthals with a single digit IQ. But then I met Cameron Forbes personally, really I did, and now I believe my grandfather.

After World War II, when I was studying in MIT, Vicky and Mandy Abad Santos (daughters of our hero Jose Abad Santos, who married two Madrigal brothers), Dolly and Neneng Buencamino (cousins of my wife and descendants of Felipe Buencamino who reportedly had General Antonio Luna assassinated) and Rosie Osmeña (daughter of President Sergio Osmeña) came by train from Mills College to Boston in dead winter. I drove them, actually I drove the car while they were pushing it, to a suburb where they were guests of W. Cameron Forbes, already 78 years of age, living alone with his sister, in a fabulous mansion fronting a polo field. He had rooms all paneled with Philippine woods, and a piano of solid narra, which sounded like a guitar trapped in a closet, because solid narra is not a good sounding board for a piano.

Cameron Forbes served us an elegant dinner. Still a bachelor (he may have been gay), Forbes wore a a tuxedo, formal monkey suit, for dinner. And the dinner was pure New England: Boston baked beans, stuffed turkey with cranberry jelly, red wine and apple pie. He had uniformed Filipino maids who were delighted to talk to us in half-forgotten Tagalog. In the girl's guest room, there was a secret door at the back of a closet that led to what Dolly Buencamino described as Bluebeard's Chamber, with lighted candles and all sorts of strange figurines. One had to light incense sticks to enter another room with a magic view of Taj Mahal in miniature.

As Governor General in1909, he governed the Philippines with vague generalities. He was a Proper Bostonian (distinct from Old Bostonians like the Cabots and Lowells) who held office properly.   Never did a more undistinguished man hold a distinguished office in a more undistinguished fashion. To promote American Business, Forbes expelled Chinese businessmen from the Philippines by the tens of thousands, by virtue of no power whatsoever legally vested in him. Forbes represented the powerful Republican "nobles" back home, whose interest was to keep the Philippines forever an American colony.   Theodore Roosevelt described Forbes as a conservative, "one who could only be bribed by money he already has." In 1921 Republican President Warren Harding sent the Wood-Forbes Mission to determine if the Philippines was ready for total independence. At the time, Filipinos held the entire legislature; five out of six of the cabinet positions; four out of nine in the Supreme Court; Attorney General, Solicitor General and all the fiscals; 53 out of 55 judges; all 893 municipal presidents; 45 out of 48 provincial governors; all justices of the peace; 97 percent of the Constabulary officers; 24 out of 28 bureau chiefs; 99 percent of the civil service. **In other words, Filipinos in effect exercised all the domestic powers of a sovereign state.**

Yet Cameron Forbes (and his colleague Leonard Wood) insisted that the Philippines was NOT ready for Independence. My grandfather Senator Don Daniel Maramba told me he was stupid. He is right, Forbes Park was named after an idiot.
December 4, 2017, UNTV

Part 9. The Romulo Urban Legend by Margarita Hamada

Salasa was an old town next to Lingayen, Pangasinan. When the Agno River began eroding its banks that bordered the town proper, the township was absorbed by a barrio, farther away, now a town called Bugallon. Salasa's cathedral and municipio managed to survive and are still standing where they had always stood.

Every February 14, the Castro family to whom I am related, invite relatives to their town fiesta. There, in their house, we are served sumptuous dishes of pork, chicken and preserved fruits, all from their backyard. After lunch, photo albums were passed around for the guests to remember their old days in that old town. Photos of Carlos P. Romulo dominated many of the albums — his baby pictures, pictures of his marriage to his first wife, Virginia Llamas, his foreign sojourns, clippings of his UN activities, etc. Why many photos of CPR?

It was in 1998 when my questions about Romulo's photos in the Castro house got answered. My mother's cousin, Antonio Canullas, 93 or 95 years old at that time, a retired public school principal and a resident of Salasa, told me this story:

Towards the close of the 19th century, two college students from the Ateneo de Manila sought refuge in Salasa to escape their enemies in Manila who wanted to kill them. One of these fugitives was Gregorio Romulo, who was from Camiling, then a town of Pangasinan. The fugitives stayed in the Castro house for more than a year, after which time, the quarrel ended in a truce and the two fugitives finally were able to leave Salasa.

Gregorio Romulo went home to Camiling, his hometown. After some time, word reached the Castros that he had married his sweetheart, Maria Peña, with whom he had no communication for more than a whole year while he was in Salasa. The Castros' close friend, Maria Bengzon, a diminutive lass, was distraught, because she was pregnant with Romulo's child. She secretly managed to let him know of her predicament. Romulo thought about it and finally, the two erstwhile lovers hatched a plan. He was willing to raise the child but could not risk hurting his new bride by admitting that he was the father. He advised her to have the child and leave it by the roadside on a day he and his wife were to pass by on their way to Lingayen where they had just opened a business, buying and selling rice. On the day appointed, the new Mrs. Romulo, while travelling in a *caromata* with her husband, heard the anguished cries of a newborn. Following her ears, she saw an infant crying its lungs out by the roadside, under the merciless sun with no adult in sight. "Stop!" she cried to the driver. "There's a poor baby abandoned by the road! What heartless mother could have done such a grievous deed as this!? "Then, turning to her husband, she alighted from the *caromata* and declared, there and then, to adopt the poor foundling and raise it as her very own. Her husband posed no objections, of course, and secretly rejoiced that his problem got beautifully solved without his indiscretion being discovered.

The child grew up in Camiling, and was taught to read and write at age 3 by Mrs. Romulo, who was impressed by his precociousness. She loved him dearly as much as she loved the children that she gave birth to in later years. Every year, around

Christmas and during the long summer, Carlos P. Romulo stayed in Salasa, playing with the town kids, among them, my uncle Antonio who distinctly remembers that Carlos had a penchant for delivering speeches in the town plaza. He'd stand on a wooden box and deliver impassioned speeches. His playmates ran around him, taunting him, saying, *"Ambaguel! Ambaguel!'*, meaning, crazy boy. I do not think Carlos P. Romulo ever knew about the details of his birth, or anything else about his mother, Maria Bengzon except her diminutive size. The Bengzons are known academicians, as Chief Justice Cesar Bengzon was, and CPR is celebrated for his cerebral accomplishments, and for his being "a dime among nickels", so the story of cousin Antonio must be true.

Larry's Comment: So easy to verify this, a match-up between a DNA test of any of Carlos P. Romulo's descendants, and a DNA test of one of Maria Bengzon's relatives, say, lawyer Ricardo Romulo and Dr. Alran Bengzon, hahaha!
November 15, 2017

Part 10. Requiem for Washington SyCip

Washington SyCip died recently at the age of 96, three years older than I am, and I wept. I wept because he is the dearest of my friends. It all started during World War II when I and my best friend and future cousin-in-law Neno Abreu, were students at the University of the Philippines, and were the favorite students of Angel Baking and Professor Gokhali, founders of the Communist Party. We saw this pretty Fil-Chinese girl Ana Yu being molested by the boys and we came to her rescue, "Listen, boys, lay off! Chinese girls are for Chinese boys," we said and became the friend and protector of Ana.

Ana and Leticia Ramos (Shahani) enrolled in famed Wellesley College near Boston, where I was a student at MIT, and I made it a point to visit them every month or so. One night in deep winter, fresh from Columbia University, Washington SyCip visited me at my dorms and introduced himself as the boyfriend of Ana Yu, thanked me for being nice to her, and began a friendship that was to endure the rest of our lives.

He was the more generous, I owe him more than he owes me. When I came back from the US, he met me, initiated me into the Jaycees, and into the faculty of the University of the East, which he and his colleagues made the business college of choice.

He introduced me to his father Don Albino Sycip, head of China Bank, who lectured me on the Golden Rule, and gave my company loans without collateral, upon Wash's guarantee that I was a good risk. I was one of the first clients of his SGV *gratis et amore*, but I paid him anyway.

When I won the bid to supply election booths, his wife's company Yutivo & Sons, raised the prices of steel angle bars, but Wash stepped in and kept the price down. My son Atom worked for him, and he offered to send him to Harvard as his scholar; I declined his offer and financed his study myself.

When my son Atom organized an offshore bank for National Bank of Chicago, Washington SyCip served in his board, as his partner Fred Velayo served in mine. I got her sister, Paz Yuchengco to be the godmother of my daughter Elvira. When Elvira set out to win two Guinness World Records for Breastfeeding, Wash Sycip insisted that his firm undertake the accounting and auditing of her efforts, without compensation. I named my daughter Rosanna after her grandmother Rosario Roensch and his wife Ana Yu.

When I needed advice or just aching for his company, all I needed to do was to ask, and he dropped his busy schedule to feed me excellent Chinese food in his private dining room. He attended all my birthday parties. All these and many more!! Live a thousand years, I could never find a more generous friend. All because I was nice to a pretty Chinese girl!!!!

He had everything, there was nothing I could do to repay him, except extolling him in my column and asking President Gloria Arroyo to give him the highest Presidential Award of Honor, the Ancient Order of Lakadula, rank of Supremo.

He is the founder of the accounting firm SyCip Gorres Velayo, the best in East Asia, and is known to the world as the Grand Old Man of Philippine Business, awarded Dr. Jose P. Rizal Award for Excellence, Lifetime Achievement Award for Public Service; The Officer's Cross of the Order of Merit by Germany; Star of the Order of Merit by Austria; Officer First Class of the Royal Order of the Polar Star, by the King of Sweden; the Golden Medallion of Professional Excellence and Business Leadership by the Professional Regulation

Commission; the 1992 Ramon Magsaysay Award for International Understanding; 1997 MAP Management Man of the Year; Accountancy Hall of Fame by the Phil. Inst. of Certified Public Accountants; He succeeded in getting the Harvard Business School to conduct special courses in the Philippines, and eventually to help set up the Asian Institute of Management, the "Harvard Business School" of Asia.

December 8, 2017

ooooo

THE HUMAN CONDITION

Part 1. Tales about UP and Tau Alpha

When the World War started on December 8, 1941, I was in second year, AB Liberal Arts in the Ateneo de Manila. When the Japanese occupied Manila they closed all schools. Ateneo, manned by American Jesuits, never re-opened during the Occupation. But the University of the Philippines did. There I enrolled in the School of Engineering, and was invited to join the Tau Alpha, Engineering fraternity, together with my best friend, Jose "Neno" Abreu Jr. I was subject to the usual initiation rites, but not very much. I found myself "protected" by Ricardo de Leon, later President of Atlantic Gulf and Pacific, Inc., and Cesar Nuguid from Famfanga. I was in the same batch with Dante Santos, later President of Philacor and member of the Agrava Commission, and I believe Vicente "Ting" Paterno, later Secretary of Trade and Industry. I myself became in time, a graduate of the Massachusetts Institute of Technology, President of the Chamber of Industries, Eisenhower Fellow, and a cabinet member in the administration of Diosdado Macapagal. Among our older brods was Beans Castro who later became a general..

The only "bad time" I got was when I was blindfolded and forced to eat a dead worm; later I found out it was only macaroni. When it was my turn to haze others, I was shocked when one-inch paddles were broken on the butts of the neophytes, silver iodide used to burn and mark their backs, and 220 volt lines dipped into the pool to make electrolytes of our new brods. I never attended an initiation rite after that. On the other hand, as soon as I left for the States, my brother Teddy enrolled in UP, joined the Tau Alpha and was given the full treatment that I actually deserved and did not get.

My favorite professors were Professor Gohkali, an Indian Filipino who taught us Chemistry, and Instructor Angel Baking, a young man with a crewcut who taught us Solid Geometry. Both were founders of the original Communist Party of the Philippines (CPP) and were involved in the *Hukbalahap* (*Hukbo ng Bayan Laban sa Hapon*, the People's Army against the Japanese) movement; later an insurgency army after the war, under Huk Supremo Ka Luis Taruc who was not a Communist but a Socialist. I remember Gohkoli so well because he was always a little tipsy. The other Professor I remember was Mr. Hilario, a classmate of my mom, who taught us English. I was about the laziest person there was, and I always tried to bamboozle my professors to tolerate my absences, and still give me good grades. My first victim was Professor Hilario. On the first day of class, I brought my album of magazine articles and radio plays that I wrote in Ateneo under Father Reuter, who was always goading his students into writing articles for popular magazines and radio plays for KZRC. After class I went up to Professor Hilario and volunteered to show him my album. The good professor looked over my literary output with polite interest, occasionally pointing out some grammatical error, dangling participles, split infinitives, double negatives, stream-of-consciousness – till I pointed out that Erskine Caldwell, Ernest Hemingway, Mark Twain and others were not averse to defying rules of grammar and idiom. I spoke of Gilbert K. Chesterton, Bernard Shaw, H. G. Wells, Hilaire Belloc, Booth Tarkington. I pointed out that James Joyce wrote one sentence that was 80 pages long. By the time I was through with him, Professor Hilario was dizzy with the thought that I read more books than he ever did. "Well, Mr. Henares," he said, "You are well read and you write very well." "Thank you," I replied, and added, "Professor, may I see YOUR album?" Professor Hilario looked at me, and said, "I see I am going to have trouble with you, Henares. You're a real pain in the ass. Tell you what, don't come to my class at all, I will just give a passing grade, 3." "Sir I deserve more than that, I deserve a perfect grade, 1. We bargained and I settled for a grade of 1.5.

Wow, I was so gratified getting my way with Professor Hilario that I plotted to do the same to my math instructor Angel Baking. Occasionally there are trick problems in math that are unsolvable by the usual means. You try and try, till you simply give up and go to sleep. Then you wake up at night, your brain alight with inspiration, "My God, why did I not think of that before?" you wonder, and solve the problem with ease. Now such problems are hard to solve but very easy to contrive. And that is exactly what I did, and I asked Baking to solve the problem in class. Baking fancied himself a ladies' man, and comported himself on the blackboard with a flourish. After he failed to solve the problem three times, I elbowed him aside, saying "I think this is the way to solve it, sir." – while the girls gave me a standing ovation. "After class, Henares," Baking whispered. And after class he hissed, *"Putang ina mo, sinadya mo yoon."* "Sir, don't get mad, I just want you to exempt me from class." *"Walang hiya ka*, there is a rule, if you're absent ten days you will fail no matter how good you are!" "Sir, you know what I do during vacation? I amuse myself by solving every problem in the book. Give me any problem in the book, even the ones at the very end, I can solve it." Angel Baking was fascinated to find I taught myself during summer and could really solve any problem in the book. His anger passed. "Tell you what," he proposed, "Just show up during mid-term and final exams, and I will give a final grade that is the average of your grades in those two exams."

The best time I had as a Tau Aphan was right after Liberation in 1945, when we went back to UP. This time the entire UP Campus on Padre Faura was razed to the ground, and we found our classes in the old College of Pharmacy. The Old Nurses Home at the corner of Padre Faura and Taft was occupied by the WACs (Women's Auxiliary Corps of the US Armed Forces). Being now a master, I commanded a neophyte to bring me to WACs' headquarters, pretend he is my master and command me to spend the next two weeks cleaning the floors of their dormitory. What I time I had! After class hours I went there to clean floors and saw the girls in various stages of undress. Some of them even asked me if I was a virgin (I was!) and teasingly bared every tantalizing square inch for me, "for an education in Anatomy," she explained. Eventually I was asked to choose the WAC that I want to remember all my life. I chose the smallest best looking one. She invited me out for a walk toward the Chemistry Laboratory, and there I had my baptism of fire on the cold stainless steel table of the lab. I'll never forget her. I corresponded with her in the USA, visited her, her husband and family. She passed away already leaving me with the memory of one of the most beautiful experiences of my life.

One day, the WAC lieutenant asked me to accompany her to the Army Kitchen, which was located in the campsite amidst the ruins of the UP campus just across the street. "I just want to check on the food they send us, it tastes funny," she explained. We came upon this army cook, a big black man sweating mud.

He was kneading dough, took a bit of the dough in each hand, and slapped them on his stomach to flatten the dough. His navel protruded out, so it made an imprint on the dough. Into that imprint he put a raisin, placed the dough on a pan, pushed the pan into the oven and baked cookies out of them.

"Horrible!" exclaimed the WAC lieutenant, "Don't you think it is simply horrible?" The negro cook answered, "Horrible? You should see the way I make the DOUGHNUTS!!" Then with a twinkle in his eye, he added, "Dirty minds, I did it with my finger!" It was the middle finger turned upwards, a typical American gesture.

A few months later I embarked on a journey to Boston, Massachusetts, bound for MIT where I continued my studies. There were no commercial planes then or even ocean liners, so I had to be content to take the month long journey on board a small Liberty Ship, along with American sailors. I was assigned a bunk, unmade with no pillows, no bed sheet. I asked my shipmate, "Where is the sheet?" He answered, "You go down the starboard side, turn right, door to the left." I did and found myself in a bathroom, with no bed sheets. I went back, a little miffed, "Hey sailor, I want a sheet, you know, like on your bed." And he exploded, "You shit on my bed, damn you, and I'll throw you overboard!"
October 2-3, 2006

Part 2. Jackie Brown, blasting nagging women into eternal silence

I always am a little nervous whenever I am called upon to address or hold a dialogue with women. My friends who notice this initial nervousness, verging on panic on my part, would advise me: "When finding yourself in the company of women, why don't you just pretend you are talking to your wife? And make it a sort of extended conversation."

Well and good, but bless her saintly soul, every time I did talk to my late wife Cecilia, it was no longer a conversation but a monologue and she did most of the talking. And the only way I could shut her mouth was to kiss her on the lips. This is something I just could not do with women who have bad breath and jealous husbands. Suddenly a light bulb lights up in a bubble above my head.

I was in a movie house watching *Jackie Brown*, starring Pam Grier, Samuel Jackson, Robert de Niro and Bridget Fonda. In the story, Samuel Jackson cooks up a scheme to bring back illegal funds, obtained from drugs and gun-running, from Mexico back into the USA. Samuel Jackson recruits a simpleton buddy of his, just released from prison, Robert de Niro, to participate in the scam along with his girfriend Bridget Fonda. Fonda, an acid head, has a proclivity for casual sex: "Wanna screw?" she asks de Niro in a middle of a perfunctory conversation, and turns her back to him while he satisfies himself, doggie style, standing up. And all the while she is trying to talk de Niro into cheating Jackson out of cash in question, overwhelming the poor inarticulate convict with her incessant chatter.

On the day of the caper, Bridget wakes up late, is dragged by de Niro to the scene of the crime where she irritates him with her nagging tongue. They received the cash in a shopping bag. Bridget tries to walk away with it, while de Niro restrains her, and pulls her toward the getaway car. All the while she talks and nags and talks and nags. "Shut up!" he hisses, and her tongue wags on, "Shut up! One more word out of you, and… " Robert de Niro, a consummate actor, conveys to the movie audience the helpless frustration every husband feels when afflicted with a nagging wife. "Shut up, not a word more," and when she continued to nag, he pulls his gun and pumps the bullets into her head and chest.

Dear friends, you should have seen how the movie audience reacted. They clapped and cheered and gave de Niro a standing ovation. The movie director Quintin Tarantino was at his best. In that brief scene he caught something universal and true – the irritation of a man, driven to the brink of violence, as he is tortured to the very edge of insanity by a nagging woman.

Every man I know who has seen the movie was moved to acknowledge the dark moments when he actually was tempted to shot his wife. Of course they do not have my finesse, I just shut up my wife with an avalanche of kisses. But it is interesting to discuss this phenomenon with my male friends and ask them to enumerate the women other than their wives whom they would gladly dispatch out of this world with a shotgun at mid-sentence of a torrent of talk.

The champion of course is economist and TV host, Winnie Monsod, who was known to blow cigarette smoke at the men while arguing with them, and interrupting them, and making faces and uttering remarks while it was their turn to speak. She was known as the Screaming Banshee and the Wicked Witch of the West.

A close second is acidic columnist, Ninez Cacho Olivares, now the editor of Tribune, who has nothing nice to say about Cory Aquino and Ramos. The third was an insistent, inconsistent spokeswoman for a present and an ex-future president Annabelle Abaya. And fourth is the wife of a Senator Pepe Diokno, full of righteous political passion. And the best commentary on them comes from one who looks like Teddy Benigno, TV host of Firing Line: "I love to have them on my show. Every time any of these women nag and contradict us on television, Larry, we get the approbation and vote of every man who has ever been nagged by his wife." That's why Firing Line needs no gun.

But the rest of us common, ordinary, run-of-the-mill, garden-variety male of the species, in the inner sanctum of our minds, dream of that supreme moment when, confronted by a nagging virago of a woman, and struggling to put one word edgewise into a raging current of non-sequiturs, we would pull out a gun and without even saying, "Shut up, one more word out of you and.." just blast her into the eternal silence of the lambs.
May 19, 1998, ISYU

Part `3. Memory Lane on Radio Amateur Night

This is Delta Uniform One November Radio Sierra, DU1 NRS, the NRS being the phonetic equivalent of my family name, Henares, with the Spanish silent h. And I speak out of the past along memory lane, being a lifetime member of the PARA (Philippine Amateur Radio Association).

What is 10 years out of the lifetime of a man? Measured in terms of the humdrum routines of everyday living, 10 years can pass like ten minutes, uncounted and unremembered. But measured in terms of friends made, of new experiences and services rendered, 10 years can pass like ten lifetimes, every minute counted and recounted in the storehouse of one's memory. Such a time occurred in the decade of the 70's for me and a group of radio amateurs in a golden age of telecommunications. We all started as a gun club, just before martial law, called Rainbow Communications, all members being enthusiasts of the amateur 2-meter band installed in our cars. We all had pseudonyms, I was Aries, and Josemari Gonzalez was Bouncer because he was quick with his fists. The Rainbow Club offered to be and was recruited as the mobile cars of the Metro Manila Police Departments, with us providing the transceivers and the armed back-up, because we were better than the policemen when it came to target shooting. We participated in police raids and riot control.

At the outset of Martial Law, our guns were confiscated so we concentrated on Ham Radio under the auspices of the Philippine Amateur Radio Association, of which Josemari served as President and I as Executive VP and editor of our official QTC magazine . We answered emergencies, including escorting pregnant women to the hospital during the curfew hours, and braved the typhoons to provide communications to the farthest reaches of the nation. I believe that was the golden age of amateur radio in the Philippines. We were able to communicate radio hams in the Soviet Union and the Eastern Europe, we talked to US Senator Barry Goldwater, the ex-Prime Minister of Malaysia Tunku Abdul Rahman and the King of Jordan. One Filipino doctor ham, Eduardo Garcia DU6EG, even directed an appendectomy operation in a tramp steamer bound for Singapore, we rescued a ship stranded in the Carolines, and we patched American soldiers during the Tet Offensive by telephone to their beloved ones in the United States. We got students from Don Bosco to teach us the Morse Code. There was only one terrible thing. We had two trusted secretaries who betrayed us. For years they pocketed the money for postage and threw our QSL cards for mailing into the basura. One of them is the niece of the NTC Commissioner at the time.

Because of Josemari, the superstar of the late late show, and my son Ronnie Henares, we were able to have as guests such celebrities as Vilma Santos, Sharon Cuneta, Boot Anson-Roa, Elizabeth Oropesa, Lorna Tolentino, and Daria Ramirez. We had a wonderful gang, many of them already passed away, among them, Golden Heart, Jose Tupas DU1JJT; our close friend Charlie Mike, Cesar Maloles Jr. DU1CM, and Earl

Hornbostel DU1AE, an American veteran who was one of the very first ham radio operators in the Philippines.

But the most interesting of all is your present president Jose Mari Gonzalez, whom we honored in 1977, thus:

To Josemari "Bouncer" Gonzalez, DUIJMG, movie hero off and on the silver screen, hi-fi buff, outdoorsman, scuba diver, DX'er rally driver, businessman, bomba exhibitionist, great lover, spoiled brat and egomaniac –

Who for many years generously donated his time, talents and resources to the PARA in exchange for one continuous gigantic ego trip, as the leading man in a true-to-life motion picture.

Taking the role of a Prince giving largesse to the multitudes, he lavished cash, the use of his magnificent equipment and the performances of his movie star friends on many PARA projects. He shows off the best amateur radio gear, the best hi-fi system and the best-looking wife. And like the movie hero that he is, he goes to the limit to prove that he can drink the greatest amount of beer, collect the most number of QSL cards, drive the fastest, dive the deepest, climb the highest, conquer the strongest man and make love to the most beautiful woman.

He is used to winning, and if defeat comes once in a while, as it comes to all mortals, he gets into a terrible tantrum, threatening to resign from the PARA, until it was pointed out that the only way he can resign a Lifetime membership is to commit suicide.

For bringing Technicolor, Cinemascope and Stereophonic Sound into our prosaic lives, Josemari Gonzalez, alias Diablo, alias Bouncer deserves this plaque in lieu of an Oscar.
November 23, 2002

Part 4. King Arthur and the Witch

Young King Arthur was ambushed and imprisoned by the monarch of a neighboring kingdom. The monarch could have killed him, but was moved by Arthur's youthful happiness. So he offered him freedom, as long as he could answer a very difficult question. Arthur would have a year to figure out the answer; if, after a year, he still had no answer, he would be killed.

The question was: What do women really want? Such a question would perplex even the most knowledgeable man, and, to young Arthur, it seemed an impossible query.

Well, since it was better than death, he accepted the monarch's proposition to have an answer by year's end. He returned to his kingdom and began to poll everybody: the princess, the prostitutes, the priests, the wise men, the court jester. In all, he spoke with everyone but no one could give him a satisfactory answer. What most people did tell him was to consult the old witch, as only she would know the answer. The price would be high, since the witch was famous throughout the kingdom for the exorbitant prices she charged.

The last day of the year arrived and Arthur had no alternative but to talk to the witch. She agreed to answer his question, but he'd have to accept her price first: The old witch wanted to marry Gawain, the most noble of the Knights of the Round Table and Arthur's closest friend! Young Arthur was horrified: she was hunchbacked and awfully hideous, had only one tooth, smelled like sewage water, often made obscene noises... He had never run across such a repugnant creature. He refused to force his friend to marry her and have to endure such a burden.

Gawain, upon learning of the proposal, spoke with Arthur. He told him that nothing was too big of a sacrifice compared to Arthur's life and the preservation of the Round Table. Hence, their wedding was proclaimed, and the witch answered Arthur's question: What a woman really wants is to be able to be in charge of her own life.

Everyone instantly knew that the witch had uttered a great truth and that Arthur's life would be spared. And so it went. The neighboring monarch spared Arthur's life and granted him total freedom.

What a wedding Gawain and the witch had! Arthur was torn between relief and anguish. Gawain was proper as always, gentle and courteous. The old witch put her worst manners on display. She ate with her hands, belched and farted, and made everyone uncomfortable. The wedding night approached: Gawain, steeling himself for a horrific night, entered the bedroom. What a sight awaited! The most beautiful woman he'd ever seen lay before him! Gawain was astounded and asked what had happened. The beauty replied that since he had been so kind to her (when she'd been a witch), half the time she would be her horrible, deformed self, and the other half, she would be her beautiful maiden self. Which would he want her to be during the day and which during the night?

What a cruel question? Gawain began to think of his predicament: During the day a beautiful woman to show off to his friends, but at night, in the privacy of his home, an old spooky witch? Or would he prefer having by day a hideous witch, but by night a beautiful woman to enjoy many intimate moments?

What would you do? What Gawain chose follows below, but don't read until you've made your own choice.

Well, Noble Gawain replied that he would let her choose for herself. Upon hearing this, she announced that she would be beautiful all the time, because he had respected her and had let her be in charge of her own life.

What is the moral of this story? The moral is that it doesn't matter if your woman is good or bad, pretty or ugly. Underneath it all, she's still a witch!

Part 5. Mating Game
An invitation to love, lust, sex and procreation

Faces are exquisite instruments of expression. Behind our facial skin lies an intricate web of muscles, 22 of them on each side of the face, especially around the eyes and the mouth, that can be called upon to produce 10,000 different expressions - - love, hate, fear, joy, ecstasy, contentment, surprise, doubt, distrust, suspicion, interest and countless other emotions.

Evolved purely for a social communication, each emotion can be further modified by the raise of an eyebrow or the slight flick of a cheek muscle to express, say, measured surprise, wild surprise, disappointed surprise, feigned surprise, etcetera.

Among these signals are formal invitations to potential mates, called flirtations. *"'Tis not a lip, or eye, we beauty call,/ but the joint force and full result of all,"* wrote Alexander Pope. On the anatomy of the face of a woman we can see the "joint force" that perpetuates the human race -- the shy smile, the bashful lowering of a gaze to one side and down, followed by a furtive look at the man's face, the unobtrusive wetting of the lips -

- the same on the face of a Tasaday tribeswoman and a sophisticated Makati secretary.

The human mate-recognition system is overwhelmingly visual. "Love comes in at the eye," wrote Yeats, and the locus of the human body that lures the eye most of all is the face -- a trait our species shares with many other primates. "It is a common Old World anthropoid ploy," says Masters. "Cercopithecoid monkeys have brightly painted faces with species-specific patterns, which they wave like flags in the forest gloom. Good old evolution tinkering away, providing new variations on a theme." Humans love to mate. The barriers between races melt away when sex is at stake. This according to James Shreeve in his article "The Neanderthal Peace" (Discover, September, 1995), which we excerpt.

The face make-up, the sexy dress, the slight touch of the hand and whole gamut of body language are there to embellish one grand design -- an invitation to love, lust, sex and procreation -- no matter how modified by layers and layers of civilized behavior, born of culture, religion, and social convention.

A universal signal sent to all is intended to be received only by a selected few. Let those beware who respond and are not appreciated, because they are likely to be accused of sexual harassment, hounded by modern society, shamed by the thought that they were called but not welcomed.

There are few ideal couples like movie stars and the jet set, destined for happiness by heaven itself, then condemned to the hell of separations, divorce and multiple marriages. The irony is that the desirable women only want desirable men and vice-versa. The educated ones, the beautiful and the handsome, the best and the brightest, the rich and the powerful, gravitate toward each other.

And the rest of humanity are left to choose from the second-best, the dregs, the leavings, the residuals, the residues. The human race is fast devolving separately into the beautiful and the ugly, the brightest and the moronic, the rich and the poor, the good and the bad, the loved and the unlovable.

The call of the wild and wet and wonderful

The perpetuation of the race of any species begins with a mating call: the call of the wild and wet and wonderful. This message will only be heard within the same species and no other. So writes James Shreeve, in an article published in the September 1995 issue of *Discover*, "The Neanderthal Peace," which we excerpt.

"It may be a chemical, sent out by the eggs of the brown alga Ascophyllum nodosum, for example, which attracts the sperm of A. nodosum and no other. It may be the color, perfume and nectar of a flower attracting insects to bring the pollen from the stamen to the pistil. Or a vaginal smell like that of a bitch in heat which attracts all the male dogs in the vicinity, but not tomcats or teen-age boys. Girls and boys of the human race recognize visual signals that call for the wild and wet and wonderful, leading to the perpetuation of the species, but only of human beings.

"A female of one species might hear the song of the male of another species," explains Judith Masters of the University of Witwatersrand , "but she won't make any response. There's no need to talk about what *prevents* her from mating with that male. She just doesn't see what all the fuss is about."

Adaptations to the local habitat may influence the evolution of the species, but not as much as any change in the mate-recognition system. A sparrow born with a slightly too short beak may or may not be able to feed its young as well as another with an average size beak, but if he can attract a mate, his kind may yet survive. But a sparrow who sings an unfamiliar song will not attract a mate and is not going to have any young at all. He will be plucked from the gene pool of the next generation, leaving no evolutionary trace of his idiosyncratic serenade. The same goes, of course, for any sparrow hen who fail to respond to potential mates singing the "correct" tune.

"The only time a species' mate recognition system will change is when something really dramatic happens," Master says. For such a drama to unfold, a population must be geographically isolated from its parents. If the population is small enough and the habitat radically different from what it was previously, even the powerful evolutionary inertia of the mate-recognition system may be overcome. This change in reproduction maybe accompanied by new adaptations to the environment. Or it may not. Either way the only shift that marks the birth of the new species is the one affecting the recognition of mates. Once the recognition threshold is crossed, there is no going back. Even if individuals from the new population and the old come to live in the same region again -- let's say in a well-trafficked corridor of fertile land linking their two continental ranges -- they will not longer view each other as potential mates."

And James Shreeve theorizes, that is the reason why the Neanderthal Man and the Cro-Magnon Man, two radically different types of humans, thought to be following each other in the sequence of evolution, were surprisingly found to be existing side by side in Spain for perhaps 50,000 years. And for all those thousands of years, the two apparently had nothing to do with each other, no sexual intercourse, no common call for the wild, wet and wonderful.
November 14, 1995

Part 6. Dear Long Lost Cousin Larry, from Nicole Henares

It is so great to finally chat with you, as I have heard so much about you from Monchie! So it was you who met my Uncle Frank all those years ago. I remember the story how he met our long lost cousins from when I was a little girl and it always intrigued me, which is why I was so happy to make that connection with Monchie over the internet. Even better, Ted's youngest daughter Cricket attends University here in San Francisco, we met in May and have become friends even, it is so neat!

I too was always interested in the Cervantes connection to the town with our name, however, alas we come from clever but humble origins out of Cordoba which is in Andalusia, a different region of Spain than Alcala de Henares. My grandfather, Nicholas (Francisco's younger brother) is very proud of being Andalusian and growled at me when I dared to suggest the possibility that we were from Alcala de Henares, which is in Segovia I believe. Somehow someone in our lineage must of been from Alcala or near the Henares river, thus adopting the name, but when I do not know.

My great grandfather Francisco, his younger brother who I believe was named Hilarion as well (I am not too sure), Francisco's wife Maria, and his young son Juan left Spain in the 1890's due to economic hardship. Spain, as you know, was not a pleasant place for the proletariat back in the 19th century.

Oppression, a cast system, a poor crop, a very corrupt Catholic church, and lack of opportunity, lack of ability to survive or progress were all motivating factors in the Henares' plans to leave Spain for America, specifically California. However it was not such a simple task to get there. Immigrants were often offered passage as steerage on steamships with the promise of work once they got to a destination.

However for the Henareses in the 1890's, no opportunity to get to America came up, but passage to and a job in the Philippines did (which promised to lead to another opportunity to get to America in time).

It is interesting to note that many Spaniards came not across the Atlantic but the Pacific to work on plantations in Hawaii after Hawaii was annexed to the United States in 1898, as my grandmother's side of the family did. I do not know exactly what the dates are when the Henareses arrived the Philippines, I think sometime around 1896 or 1895 before the 1898 revolution. I do know that when the passage and work to California came up, not too long after they arrived, again before 1898, Francisco, his wife and son departed, but Hilarion stayed behind as he had fallen in love and married a Philippine lady -- very romantic if you think about it! I have to get going to work. I teach high school English here in San Francisco. but I will be sure to write more of the Henares family saga of the California years later! All the best.
December 2003

Part 7. Spanish habits

Spaniards have an unusual schedule of eating and sleeping. At 9 am they wake up and have a light breakfast, their smallest meal called *Desayuno*. During the following hours they continue to eat finger foods, which they call *Tapas* (no meat, nothing to do with our Filipino tapa). In the Philippines we used to call this mid-morning snack *Segundo Almuerzo*.

Long after at 2 pm, they take off for a long lunch break which lasts up to 5:30 pm, during which they eat their largest meal of several courses (*La Comida*), and go to sleep taking what is known as a *Siesta*.

After *siesta*, they take *La Merienda*, and then really and finally go to work until 9 pm, when they take *La Cena*, a dinner smaller than *La Comida*.

Spaniards are inveterate night owls, usually going out doing the town, and crawling back home for a bit of night cap called *Churros*, featuring fritters and thick chocolate. To bed at midnight and wake up at 9 am.

Wow, that adds up to 6 meals a day, and 3 ½ hours of work daily, 11 ½ hours of sleep a day.

Spaniards eat more and work less than any people in the entire world. Even today, during tourist season when their economy is most productive, they just rent out their houses and go on tour outside their country. And most of blame for their lazy habits, they place on their woeful experiences during their Civil War in the 1930s (IGMG, *i google mo gago*). Not true. Those Spanish habits have been with us in the Philippines for centuries.

Spaniards have a single digit IQ, they do not believe in science and burn their intellectuals at the stake, because they already have the ultimate truth in the Catholic Church. Their greatest fear is not to go to hell, but to be cuckolded by their wives (*Pendejo!*). Yet they are haughty, the proudest in Europe, with the least reason for being so.

How did Spain turn out the laziest and most unproductive people in the planet?

Well, in the 14th Century they were the greatest nation on the face of the earth, a pioneering force in the Age of Discovery. They sponsored the discovery of America by Christopher Columbus; they sponsored the trip of Magellan to the Philippines, and Juan Sebastian Elcano's circumnavigation of the globe.

At its height of the Empire, Spaniards owned the entire western part of what is now the United States, and all of Central and South America. They were able to steal the gold of the Aztecs, the Mayans and the Incas – tons and tons of gold which they brought back to Spain.

They had more gold than there were goods available for sale. This brought about a spiraling inflation that ruined their economy. Finally, they decided that since they have more gold than any other country, they would not manufacture what they needed, they would just buy the best that the world would offer.

Thus, they missed the Industrial Revolution. They just waxed fat and lazy on the gold they stole from the Indians They ate 6 meals a day and worked only 3 ½ hours daily and slept 12 midnight to 9 am plus a siesta from 3 pm to 5:30 pm – a total of 11 ½ hours.
August 2016

Part 8. The Fourth Age of Man

In our Book 12, Rise and Fall, we wrote of the Three Ages of Man, as an individual -- childhood, adulthood and old age; as a species – a time marked by Stability, then Progress, then Social Chaos.

We write now of the Fourth Age of Man in the time of the Internet, which dwells primarily in his mind, evolving from a mindset that is local and linear, to a mindset that is global and exponential. Let me explain. For millenniums, as we humans evolved, everything that affected us was within a day's walk and changes happened in small increments, local and linear. Today everything is happening so fast and on a worldwide scale that it befuddles the mind, the challenges are both global and exponential.

In 1996, Eastman Kodak, a hundred-plus year old company was at the top of its game, with $28 billion capitalization, with 140,000 employees, and a brand known around the world. Twenty years earlier, in 1976, an employee named Stephen Sasson invented the digital camera in the Kodak laboratory, and we can only imagine what happened when he brought it to the Board of Directors' meeting, saying, "Here is the future of Kodak!"

The Board answered, "Are you kidding? It is a toy for kids. Kodak makes high resolution images, and this thing makes 12 black-and-white images at a low 0.01 megapixel resolution."

Kodak ignored Sasson; and so in 2012 Kodak filed for Chapter 11 bankruptcy, with a residual 17,000 employees.

In that same year a company called Instagram with 13 employees making digital cameras, was purchased for $1 billion by Facebook. Here was a linear-thinking company being displaced by exponential technologies.

What is the difference between linear and exponential? If you were to walk 30 steps in meters on a linear scale,

1,2,3,4,5… you'll end up 30 meters away at the back of the room.

If you do the same thing on an exponential scale, 1,2,4,8,16,32… after 30 steps, you will have traveled 1,073,741,842 meters, more than a billion meters, 26 times around the earth. The difference is between Man and Superman. The difference is called the Period of Disruption, from 1976 when the digital camera was invented to 2012 when Kodak went bankrupt.

Man's brainpower is measured by his computational skill. Such a skill was enhanced first by electro-mechanical means like the Adding Machine, then by electro-magnetic means like the Relay, then by the Vacuum tube, then by the Transistor.

It was when the Integrated Circuit (IC) came into being that man's computational skill went exponential, doubling every 18 months, as Gordon Moore, head of Intel predicted.

In 2012, a $1000 computer doing a hundred million (10^8) calculations per second (the same rate as the brain of an insect does) predicted that by 2014 it will have the brain of a mouse (10^{11}), that today in 2016 the brain of a man (10^{16} calculations per second), and that ultimately in the year 2040, it will have the collective brains of the entire population of the world (10^{26} calculations per second).

That is still far from the mind of God, which scientists calculate to be 10^{144} calculations per second, the chances of a blind person finding one particular grain of sand from all the beaches of the world, or the chances of winning a mega-lotto a thousand consecutive times betting with the same number, or the chances that life will evolve from a chance explosion of the Big Bang 13.8 billion years ago.

Will this growth go on forever? Not on your life, there is what is known as the Technology S Curve. It starts very very slow, in negligible increments, then at the "kneeling knee-point", it accelerates very very fast and then at the "shoulder point" it slows down and practically plateaus flat, forming a slanting S-curve. Then another technology takes it to a higher level, and so on and so on. It is possible to go on and on, but not forever.

In 1958, 2 transistors were incorporated in the first Integrated Circuit, 7/16 inch in size; in 1971, Intel 400 had 2,300 transistors in its IC, a speed of .00074 Gigahertz, and cost $1 per transistor; in 2012, Nvidia GPU contained 7.1 billion transistors, a speed of 7 GHz and the cost of $0.0000001 per transistor.

In 1976 Sassoon's first digital camera had a resolution of 0.01 megapixels, weighed 3.75 lbs and cost $10,000; the Digital Camera of 2014, had a 10 megapixel resolution, weighed 0.03 lbs and cost $10 -- 1000 times the resolution, 1000 times lighter, 1000 times cheaper, 1,000,000,000 times better.

In the 1960s, the first ICBM navigational system that took us to the moon, cost $50 million, and weighed 50 lbs; today an Accelerator costs 30 cents, the Gyroscope costs $1 and both fit in your pocket; today molecular machines, free and embedded, are woven into your clothing, measuring every motion of your arms and legs. The first commercial GPS receiver in 1981 weighed 53 lbs, cost $119,900 and cannot fit on the dashboard of your car; in 2010, a single chip GPS receiver cost less than $5, and fits in your pocket.

I want to tell you of the **6Ds** Exponential Framework.

The first **1D** is that anything that becomes **Digitized** enters exponential growth. What does digitized mean? Well anything converted to ones and zeroes is being digitized.

And when it is digitized it enters a period of **Deceptive (2D)** growth. The .01 megapixel camera, remember, went to .02 megapixels, .04, .08, .16 megapixels, but they all look like zeroes.

After that slow period of growth, it accelerates faster and faster until it becomes **Disruptive (3D)**, then it **Dematerializes (4D)**, **Demonetizes (5D)**, and finally **Democratizes (6D)**. Let me explain what these mean.

When something enters a rapid **disruptive period**, it becomes **dematerialized**, it becomes so small it fits in your pocket, as did the GPS that sits on your dashboard, as did your record collection after Spotify, as did high resolution video cameras, still cameras, games, everything that have physically dematerialized.

When they do, they become **demonetized**. Demonetization is powerful and dangerous. So iTunes demonetized the record store.; Skype demonetized the long distance phone; Amazon the bookstore; Google the research library; Ebay the local store. And Craigslist decimated the newspaper industry, took the money out of classified ads, and put it in somebody else's pocket. And when something gets **dematerialized** and **demonetized**, it also becomes small enough and cheap enough to be placed in your smart phone *gratis et amore*.

It then becomes **Democratized**, and here is where the marketplace explodes. By 2016, 300 million handsets were sold in Africa. Who would have thought that one of Google's biggest markets in the world for Androids would be Africa?

The world population in 2016 reached 7.3 billion, 49.2% or 3.6 billion already connected online.

This internet penetration was 6% in 2000, 23% in 2010, 49.2% in 2016, and projected to be 75% of the estimated population of 7.7 billion in 2020. That's a market of 5.8 billion four years from today.

What happens when 3.6 billion become 7.7 billion internet users in 4 years? That translates to 5.1 billion more people who never bought anything before. They are a brand new generation of consumers, a brand new generation of creators, a brand new generation of inventors.

What problems do they have to solve if they create new products and services that they will plow back to us?

They will trigger I believe the greatest epic era of innovation ever. New markets will bring tens of trillions of dollars to the rest of us.

We pause to give a few critical insights on this Fourth Age of Man.

The **First** is that the only constant is change and the rate of change is increasing. It is not slowing down.

The **Second** insight is that you either disrupt your own company/products, or somebody else will. Standing still, equals death. If you are making a decent profit margin, someone is going to disrupt you and the disruption is no longer coming from the multinational on the other side of the planet, it is the exponential entrepreneur on the Internet.

The **Third** insight then is this: your competition is no longer the multinational overseas; it is the explosion of exponentially empowered entrepreneurs who have the tools to disrupt you, and drive you to bankruptcy from anywhere on the planet.

Come then, abandon the local and linear mindset. Adopt the global and exponential frame of mind. Join us and enter the Fourth Age of Man.
August 2016

Part 9. Why are Jews so powerful? by Dr Farrukh Saleem

There are only 14 million Jews in the world; seven million in the Americas, five million in Asia, two million in Europe and 100,000 in Africa. For every single Jew in the world there are 100 Muslims. Yet, Jews are more than a hundred times more powerful than all the Muslims put together.

Ever wondered why?

Jesus of Nazareth was Jewish. Albert Einstein, the most influential scientist of all time and TIME magazine's "Person of the Century", was a Jew. Sigmund Freud -- id, ego, and superego -- the father of psychoanalysis was a Jew. So were Karl Marx, Paul Samuelson and Milton Friedman.

Here are a few other Jews whose intellectual output has enriched the whole humanity: Benjamin Rubin gave humanity the vaccinating needle. Jonas Salk developed the first polio vaccine. Albert Sabin developed the improved live polio vaccine. Gertrude Elion gave us a leukemia fighting drug. Baruch Blumberg developed the vaccination for Hepatitis B. Paul Ehrlich discovered a treatment for syphilis (a sexually transmitted disease). Elie Metchnikoff won a Nobel Prize in infectious diseases.

Bernard Katz won a Nobel Prize in neuromuscular transmission. Andrew Schally won a Nobel in endocrinology (disorders of the endocrine system; diabetes, hyperthyroidism). Aaron Beck founded Cognitive Therapy (psychotherapy to treat mental disorders, depression and phobias). Gregory Pincus developed the first oral contraceptive pill. George Wald won a Nobel for furthering our understanding of the human eye. Stanley Cohen won a Nobel in embryology (study of embryos and their development). Willem Kolff came up with the kidney dialysis machine.

Over the past 105 years, 14 million Jews have won 15-dozen Nobel Prizes while only three Nobel Prizes have been won by 1.4 billion Muslims (other than Peace Prizes).

Why are Jews so powerful?

Stanley Mezor invented the first micro-processing chip; Leo Szilard developed the first nuclear chain reactor; Peter Schultz, optical fibre cable; Charles Adler, traffic lights; Benno Strauss, stainless steel; Isador Kisee, sound movies; Emile Berliner, telephone microphone and Charles Ginsburg, videotape recorder.

Famous financiers in the business world who belong to Jewish faith include Ralph Lauren (Polo), Levis Strauss (Levi's Jeans), Howard Schultz (Starbuck's), Sergey Brin (Google), Michael Dell (Dell Computers), Larry Ellison (Oracle), Donna Karan (DKNY), Irv Robbins (Baskin & Robbins) and Bill Rosenberg (Dunkin' Donuts).

Richard Levin, President of Yale University, is a Jew. So are Henry Kissinger (American secretary of state), Alan Greenspan (fed chairman under Reagan, Bush, Clinton and Bush), Joseph Lieberman, Madeleine Albright American secretary of state), Maxim Litvinov (USSR foreign Minister), David Marshal (Singapore's first chief minister), Isaac Isaacs (governor-general of Australia), Benjamin Disraeli (British statesman and author), Yevgeny Primakov (Russian PM), Jorge Sampaio (president of Portugal), Herb Gray (Canadian deputy PM), Pierre Mendes (French PM), Michael Howard (British home secretary), Bruno Kreisky (Chancellor of Austria) and Robert Rubin (former American secretary of treasury).

In the media, famous Jews include Wolf Blitzer (CNN), Barbara Walters (ABC News), Eugene Meyer (Washington Post), Henry Grunwald (editor-in-chief Time), Katherine Graham (publisher of The Washington Post), Joseph Lelyyeld (Executive editor, The New York Times), and Max Frankel (New York Times).

Can you name the most beneficent philanthropist in the history of the world? The name is George Soros, a Jew, who has so far donated a colossal $4 billion most of which has gone as aid to scientists and universities around the world. Second to George Soros is Walter Annenberg, another Jew, who has built a hundred libraries by donating an estimated $2 billion.

At the Olympics, Mark Spitz set a record of sorts by winning seven gold medals. Lenny Krayzelburg is a three- time Olympic gold medalist. Spitz, Krayzelburg and Boris Becker are all Jewish.

Did you know that Harrison Ford, George Burns, Tony Curtis, Charles Bronson, Sandra Bullock, Billy Crystal, Woody Allen, Paul Newman, Peter Sellers, Dustin Hoffman, Michael Douglas, Ben Kingsley, Kirk Douglas, William Shatner, Jerry Lewis and Peter Falk are all Jewish?

As a matter of fact, Hollywood itself was founded by a Jew. Among directors and producers, Steven Spielberg, Mel Brooks, Oliver Stone, Aaron Spelling (Beverly Hills 90210), Neil Simon (The Odd Couple), Andrew Vaina (Rambo 1/2/3), Michael Man (Starsky and Hutch), Milos Forman (One flew over the Cuckoo's Nest), Douglas Fairbanks (The Thief of Baghdad) and Ivan Reitman (Ghostbusters) are all Jewish.

To be certain, Washington is the capital that matters and in Washington the lobby that matters is The American Israel Public Affairs Committee, or AIPAC. Washington knows that if PM of Israel Ehud Olmert were to discover that the earth is flat, AIPAC will make the 109th Congress pass a resolution congratulating Olmert on his discovery.

William James Sidis, with an IQ of 250-300, is the brightest human who ever existed. Guess what faith did he belong to?

So, why are Jews so powerful? Answer: Education.

Why are Muslims so powerless? There are an estimated 1,476,233,470 Muslims on the face of the planet: one billion in Asia, 400 million in Africa, 44 million in Europe and six million in the Americas. Every fifth human being is a Muslim; for every single Hindu there are two Muslims, for every Buddhist there are two Muslims and for every Jew there are one hundred Muslims.

Ever wondered why Muslims are so powerless? Here is why: There are 57 member-countries of the Organization of Islamic Conference (OIC), and all of them put together have around 500 universities; one university for every three million Muslims. The United States has 5,758 universities and India has 8,407. In 2004, Shanghai Jiao Tong University compiled an "Academic Ranking of World Universities", and intriguingly, not one university from Muslim-majority states was in the top-500.

As per data collected by the UNDP, literacy in the Christian world stands at nearly 90 per cent and 15 Christian-majority states have a literacy rate of 100 per cent. A Muslim-majority state, as a sharp contrast, has an average literacy rate of around 40 per cent and there is no Muslim-majority state with a literacy rate of 100 per cent. Some 98 per cent of the "literates" in the Christian world had completed primary school, while less than 50 per cent of the "literates" in the Muslim world did the same. Around 40 per cent of the "literates" in the Christian world attended university while no more than two per cent of the "literates" in the Muslim world did the same.

Muslim-majority countries have 230 scientists per one million Muslims. The US has 4,000 scientists per million and Japan has 5,000 per million. In the entire Arab world, the total number of full-time researchers is 35,000 and there are only 50 technicians per one million Arabs (in the Christian world there are up to 1,000 technicians per one million). Furthermore, the Muslim world spends 0.2 per cent of its GDP on research and development, while the Christian world spends around five per cent of its GDP.

Conclusion: The Muslim world lacks the capacity to produce knowledge.

Daily newspapers per 1,000 people and number of book titles per million are two indicators of whether knowledge is being diffused in a society. In Pakistan, there are 23 daily newspapers per 1,000 Pakistanis while the same ratio in Singapore is 360. In the UK, the number of book titles per million stands at 2,000 while the same in Egypt is 20.

Conclusion: The Muslim world is failing to diffuse knowledge.

Exports of high technology products as a percentage of total exports are an important indicator of knowledge application. Pakistan's exports of high technology products as a percentage of total exports stands at one per cent.. The same for Saudi Arabia is 0.3 per cent; Kuwait, Morocco, and Algeria are all at 0.3 per cent while Singapore is at 58 per cent.

Conclusion: The Muslim world is failing to apply knowledge.

Why are Muslims powerless? Because they aren't producing knowledge. Why are Muslims powerless? Because they aren't diffusing knowledge. Why are Muslims powerless? Because they aren't applying knowledge.

And, the future belongs to knowledge-based societies.

Interestingly, the combined annual GDP of 57 OIC-countries is under $2 trillion. America, just by herself, produces goods and services worth $12 trillion; China $8 trillion, Japan $3.8 trillion and Germany $2.4 trillion (purchasing power parity basis). Oil rich Saudi Arabia, UAE, Kuwait and Qatar collectively produce goods and services (mostly oil) worth $500 billion; Spain alone produces goods and services worth over $1 trillion, Catholic Poland $489 billion and Buddhist Thailand $545 billion. (Muslim GDP as a percentage of world's GDP is fast declining).

All they do is shout to Allah the whole day and blame everyone else for their multiple failures.

By the way, this article was written by a Muslim columnist from Pakistan!!!

Comment: *Larry Henares here saying that the main reason the Jews are so intelligent is that in the 2,000 years of their Diaspora, all the persecutions, all the pogroms, all the concentration camps they have been subjected to by the Romans, Christians, Muslims, and the Teutonic race (the Germans, Anglo-Saxons, Dutch, with their notions of racial superiority), simply eliminated the unfit, the stupid, the weak among the Jews, leaving only the strong and the brilliant in the gene pool to carry on. The Jews are by far the best and the brightest, leaving in far behind in second place the Asiatics, poor third the whites, poor fourth the Latinos, further down the blacks who are better athletes and entertainers than all the others, while the Jewish cousins, fellow Semites, the Arabs and most of the African blacks, occupy the cellar.*
May 26-28, 2010

Part 10. War

I was invited to speak before the grade school class of my youngest grandson Vigo Angeles, composed of children of 11 years, 80 years younger than I am at 91 years, with this Caveat from his mother Rosanna, who texted, "Questions are: (1) How did the Japanese enter the Philippines? (2) Why did they want to colonize us? (3) How did they treat us? (4) Did they make us learn their language? Audience are Grade 5 students as innocent as Vigo. No bad words or sex please. Share experiences during the Japanese Occupation."

I answered the four questions of course.

(1) After attacking Pearl Harbor on December 7, 1941, the Japanese bombed the US airplanes in a surprise raid on Clark Field on December 8, landed in Lingayen Gulf, occupied Open City Manila, defeated the US forces in Bataan and Corregidor, and ruled the Philippines from !942 to 1945.

(2) The immediate objective was to secure access to the oil of Indonesia under the Dutch; their professed ultimate objective was to establish an Asian Co-Prosperity Sphere under the leadership of Japan.

(3) They marched Filipino and American prisoners of war in a "Death March" from Bataan to Tarlac. At first they treated us civilians like their own people, enforcing strict discipline, by slapping people not following rules; that did not sit well among Filipinos not used to be treated this way. From the outset, Filipinos mounted a guerrilla warfare, which prompted the Japanese to arrest and torture suspected guerrilleros. When the Americans returned, the Japanese in the Battle of Manila went into frenzy of massacring non-combatants that resulted in the deaths of a hundred thousand Filipinos.

(4) No, the Japanese tried but failed to make us learn their language. The upside was that they forced us to sing our national anthem, not in English but in our own Pilipino language.

That's it, my assignment was over in less than ten minutes, leaving me a lot of time to put the subject in perspective. I added that actually Filipinos have been involved in wars with many other nations, among whom were North Korea, China and Vietnam in recent memory, Spain which colonized us for 377 years (1521-1898); the United States which colonized us for 48 years (1898-1946), and violated our independence for another 45 years (1946 to 1991 when we told them to take out their bases), a total of 93 years of exploitation; the Japanese Occupation was only for 3 years (1942-1945); a fellow Filipino tyrannized us for 14 years of Martial Law (1772-1986; China sent her people here for a thousand years, long before that Spaniards ever came, only to be absorbed into our population (10% of our blood is Chinese) and by their industry and business practices, practically bound us with their brand of Commercial Colonization.

We despise the Chinese although they did us more good than harm. We blame the Spaniards although they treated us better than themselves; they spared us the Holy Inquisition and involvement in the Wars of the Spanish Succession and the Napoleonic Wars, taxed us less and gave us the benefit of the Galleon trade. We worship the Americans who treated us worse than the Japanese did, killing a thousand men, women and children down to ten years of age for every American soldier we killed, subjected us to Zona and the water-cure, and abused our independence with McCarthyist witch-hunts and Low Level Conflicts, interfered with our elections, and prevented us from industrializing. We hated the Japs but forgave them. And we totally forgot what Marcos did to us, as his son Bongbong tries to move back to Malacanang. ###

Now let's move our perspective to a view of the world. During the 10,000 years before Christ was born, Civilization was born, with the Greatness that was Egypt, the Glory that was Greece, the Grandeur that was Rome, and the Wonder that is China. Egypt lasted 3,000 years from 3100 BC up to Alexander the Great in 332 BC, bringing Agriculture and Architecture into being. Greece lasted for 500 years, from 800 to 300 BC, giving us Philosophy, Art, Science, Democracy. Rome lasted 1,300 years from 800 BC to 500 AD, giving us Engineering, Public Works and Roman Law. China lasted 4,000 years from 2070 BC (Qia Dynasty) to 1911 AD (Sun Yat Sen) – amazing! China antedated Ancient Greece and Rome by more than a thousand years and still exists, bringing Technical Innovations and a rational way of life.

During those 10,000 years wars were fought by professional armies, according to fixed rules of engagement, extolling personal bravery and gallantry, and none of the hatred and cruelty imposed by religious bigotry and racial prejudice. Throughout those times, Mother-directed Family-oriented Gods reigned, devoid of bigotry and aversion to sex, tolerant in their acceptance of other gods into their pantheon. Egypt had the cult of Isis with over 2,000 gods starting from Ra, the sun god. Greece and Rome had a family of 12 Olympians, headed by Zeus and Jupiter, and 30 minor gods or group of gods. India and China had no gods, only two Great Teachers, Buddha and Confucius. Under such Gods, without religious hatreds, civilizations prospered in comparative peace for many centuries, nay for milleniums.

According to historians, Judaism and its two derivatives, Christianity and Islam, are Father-directed, alpha-male-based religions, and as such are intolerant of other religions, bigoted with aversion to sex, and look upon women as inferior, and objects of temptation to sin. Worshipping the same one God - Jehovah, Yaweh, the Holy Trinity and Allah – they nevertheless, turned against each other and against their own kind in an orgy of Inquisitions, burning at the stake, Crusades, Jihads and holy wars. The elimination of the Mother Principle was profoundly unsettling on human civilization and led straight to the Dark Ages. The two millenniums that constituted the Christian era, was replete with wars of incredible cruelty and religious and racial hatred, of which the worst were perpetuated by the Christians which persecuted the Jews, made war on the Muslims, and splintered bloodily into thousands of sects. The most cruel of the Christians have been the White Race, with its insatiable greed and notions of racial superiority – that motivated them to conquer other races with the cross and the sword, enslaved the blacks, massacred the indigenous races for their gold and for their lands, and poisoned the entire Chinese race with opium.

Less bloodthirsty are the Muslims who had their Golden Age when the West was mired in the Dark Ages, and gave us advances in Arts, Astronomy, and Mathematics (including the Arabic numerals). They welcomed Jews and Christians alike into Jerusalem, their ancestral domain. That was not enough for the Christians who mounted 9 crusades (including one composed of children!) and massacred 40,000 Muslims in Jerusalem, raped women, and smashed the skulls of children against walls. God was so incensed, he sent the Bubonic Plague to Europe, and killed 25 million of its population. Arab teachers peacefully gave us Filipinos their Muslim religion, Spaniards gave us the cross with the sword. Only in modern times did the Muslims retaliate with terrorist attacks. Can you blame them?   Over two centuries, the West cruelly exploited them for their oil, and expiated Germany's sins against the Jews, by carving out Israel out of Arab lands; then forbidding the Arabs from making nuclear bombs while giving Israel all the bombs it needs. That my children is the right perspective on the wars that engulf the world.

The fault lies in the religious bigotry and racial prejudice of the Christian white-trash.

The Catholic Church in particular was imposed upon the world for 14 centuries of its 20-century existence, under a fraudulent document called *Constitutum Constantini,* Donation of Constantine, which conferred upon the church, temporal power over the western world, while telling of cities that did not exist at the time of Emperor Constantine of the Roman Empire. But Christianity did bring us the Renaissance, the Age of Discovery, the Age of Reason, and two great revolutions that profoundly affected human society: The French Revolution and The Socialist Revolution. The French Revolution challenged the Divine Right of Kings and advanced the human rights of all human beings – as distinguished from the American "Revolution" and the Greek Ideal, which denied the rights of slaves -- and the right of all citizens to self-determination and self-government.

The Socialist Revolution of Karl Marx, challenged the proposition that "any one pursuing his own self-interest, pursues the interest of all," the main dictum of the Capitalist System, and goes back to the Christian religious orders and communes, by which "from each according to his talents, to each according to his needs." Socialism came into being to counter harsh Capitalist practices like monopoly and inhumanity to the working class; child and women protection, the minimum wage, progressive taxation, social welfare and medicare are all Socialist ideas. Communism failed because its Socialism was imposed harshly and tyrannically. Capitalism survived because it adapted to Socialist concerns. The ideal state is the golden mean between the two systems, the socialist-capitalistic governments of the Scandinavian countries, Sweden and Norway where there are no rich or poor, only the middle class, with safety nets from the cradle to the grave -- not the United States, with its imperfect electoral system, its religious nuts, its gun freaks, its hillbillies, rednecks and white trash. Yet we must admit the Americans gave us the Nuclear Age, the Race to the Stars, the Biological Revolution and Internet.

So, what does the future hold for us, we who are Asians of the Asia Pacific Rim? The world of the future should be a world of slow population growth, widespread development and dwindling natural resources. In such a world, where will

humanity get the resources to feed itself? Not from outer space and the planets, but from the last frontier on earth – The Sea. The sea comprises three-fourth of the surface of our planet, the ultimate repository of all our resources. As the water cycle revolves from water vapor to rain, the rain water washes away the resources of the land and deposits them into the sea, and rising again as water vapor, leaves such resources forever in the sea. On land, Man has already advanced from a hunter to a farmer, to a skilled industrial worker. In the sea, Man is still the hunter-fisherman. Here in the sea, the man of the future will have undersea farms where he will harvest undersea crops and plankton that can feed his people beyond their wildest dreams. Here in the sea the man of the future will set up undersea grazing areas, where he can domesticate fishes and marine animals, fenced in by sound waves, just like he does with cattle and chicken. Here in the sea, with energy stored by the sun like a huge battery, by the heat differential between the surface and the depths, by the rise and fall of the tides, the man of the future can generate the energy he needs without end. But the sea can only be exploited only on the shallow continental shelf. Asian nations stand astride the warmest continental shelf in the world, starting from the South China Sea, south to Borneo, Malaysia and Indonesia, north to Batanes, and east to the Philippines and the Marianas Trench, the deepest on earth. This is where our ultimate destiny lies, our very own resource by the Law of the Sea and the Archipelago Principle.
March 28-30, 2016. UNTV

Part 11. Florence Foster Jenkins
Her last words: *"People may say I cannot sing, but they cannot say I did not sing."*
Her last song: *When I have sung my songs to you, I'll sing no more;*

> *T'would be a sacrilege to sing at another door;*
> *We've worked so hard to hold our dreams, just you*
and I;

> *I could not share them all again, I'd rather die,*
> *With just the thought that we had loved so well, so true,*
> *That I could never sing again,*
> *That I could never never sing again, except to you!*

The singer's story is the inspiration for a new moving movie starring Meryl Streep. It sounds like a farce: in the new movie *Florence Foster Jenkins,* out Friday, Meryl Streep plays the eponymous socialite, a woman whose singing voice is so bad it's good. But Jenkins was a real person—and if she were alive today, she'd probably be going viral on YouTube.

She was born in 1868 into a wealthy family in Wilkes-Barre, Penn.; her father was a lawyer and a member of the state legislature. When her parents died, she inherited enough money to take voice lessons, put out five recordings and host an annual concert at the Ritz-Carlton in New York City throughout the 1930s and 40s, as well as other performances in Newport, R.I.; Washington, D.C.; and Boston, according to the *American National Biography.* Founding a Verdi club helped her grow an audience, as did the work of her manager and longtime partner, the actor St. Clair Bayfield (played by Hugh Grant in the film). As the above LIFE magazine photo shows, she hosted recitals at her home in New York City's Seymour hotel, where she is said to have also kept guests entertained with a bathtub of potato salad and a collection of dining room chairs that she claimed Americans had died sitting in, according to a new biography of the amateur singer released with the film's script.

From a 1934 TIME review of Florence Foster Jenkins in concert:

Mrs. Jenkins appeared in flame-colored velvet, with yellow ringlets piled high on her head. For a starter she picked Brahms' *Die Mainacht*, subtitled on her gift program as "O singer, if thou canst dream, leave this song unsung." With her hands clasped to her heart she passed on to *Vergeblitches Standchen*, which she labeled "The Serenade in Vain."

The audience, as Mrs. Jenkins' audiences invariably do, behaved very badly. In the back of the hall, men and women in full evening dress made no attempt to control their laughter. Dignified gentlemen sat with their handkerchiefs stuffed in their mouths and tears of mirth streaming down their cheeks. But Mrs. Jenkins went bravely on. For a Spanish group she wore a mantilla, carried a big feather fan, undertook a few little dancing steps to convey more spirit. While she was getting her breath, the Percarella chamber group played Dvorak's Quintet and cameramen photographed the happy laughing faces in the audience.

Mrs. Jenkins' voice was a little tired but back she came in blue & cream satin, a rhinestone stomacher and a rhinestone tiara. Cine-men turned their cameras on her while she struggled with the *Vissi d'Arte* from *Tosca*. Last year she sang a flower song while tossing roses into the audience. In her excitement the basket slipped from her hand, hit an old man on the head. Last week she repeated the flower song, pleased her friends by again hurling the basket.

October 2016

Part 12. Speech at Cristalle's Wedding, September 8, 2016, Manila Peninsula

The exchange of words between Atom and Vicki has always been scintillating and laced with wit and humor. My favorite is one that happened even before they were married.

VICKI: Tell you a secret.

ATOM: Go ahead.

VICKI: You won't get mad or anything?

ATOM: No, I promise.

VICKI: Well all my friends say you are so handsome. But between you and me, I don't think you are handsome at all. Charming perhaps, but certainly not handsome.

ATOM: I don't think that is something to get mad about. I want to tell you a secret too, okay?

VICKI: I know. I know. You don't think I am good-looking either, right?

ATOM: On the contrary, darling, I think you are awfully good-looking!

VICKI: What is the problem?

ATOM: Well, all my friends say you are ugly!

At this point, Vicki aimed a karate kick at Atom's groin. Later her father constitutional delegate Ike Belo would remonstrate, "*Hija, hija,* you can't hit him there. Remember he will be the father of your children." Vicki could not have hit Atom very hard because Vicki bore him two children, Quark and Cristalle, my eldest granddaughter in the Philippines.

I have seen the best of ballerinas, Margot Fonteyn of the Royal Ballet, Maya Plisetskaya of Bolshoi, Moira Shearer, Natalia Makarava -- but none impressed me more than Cristalle as a ballerina who was beautiful, stately, and enchanting, with floating fluid elegance, and who danced with such artistry and versatility that she received a standing ovation punctuated with shouts and screams of "Bravo, Cristalle, Bravo!"

Well, what do you expect? Cristalle was my seven-year-old grandchild in her first ballet recital, and there were at least 12 family members in the audience, eyes focused exclusively on her, cheering her on. She may have looked liked Olive Oyl or Betty Boop to others, but to us she looked like Isadora Duncan and Cyd Charisse combined.

At the age of 17, Cristalle was already the favorite Fairy Godmother of her younger cousins, and highly popular among her classmates, who looked upon her as Secretary of Transportation whose van was available to bring them anywhere anytime. On elocution contests she won hands down because she spoke Shakespeare, Mark Antony (O pardon me thou bleeding piece of earth), Hamlet (To be or not to be, that is the question), Macbeth (Tomorrow and tomorrow and tomorrow). On July 12, 1999 for English Class, 4th year High, the class was asked to write their biodata, Cristalle wrote in perfect Shakespearean poetry, in iambic pentameter, no less:

I am Cristalle, the Goddess of Light, daughter of Atom the God of Maximum Destruction, sister of Quark the God of Minimum Destruction, and niece of the Queen Goddess Juno. My mother is Queen Victoria, Goddess of the Epidermis, who has given me a skin of ultimate perfection, translucent as alabaster, stained with rose petals. I have three grandfathers, one more than anyone else, a magic three like the Holy Trinity, to give me strength and wisdom: King Hilarious, the God of Laughter, Harbinger of Happiness; King Henry Belo the Lawmaker; and Emperor Augustus Cancio the Peacemaker. I have inherited the beauty of my grandmothers St. Cecilia Lichauco, patroness of music, and Florencia Belo, the Goddess of Flowers, and Imelda Cancio the Immaculate Concepcion. I am endowed with breasts that rise like twin peaks as perfect as Mt. Mayon, smoldering with the inner fire of passion all ready to erupt!

I am Cristalle, the Goddess of Light. I bring Light to the Universe, the Light of Knowledge, the Light of Wisdom, the Light of Hope and Faith, the Light of Love and Life itself. I bring the

Light of Logic to the mind, crystal clear like my name. In my name, men conquered their ignorance, and marched forth to create civilizations that advance the progress of Man himself. In my name, men conquered the evil within, and brought peace and prosperity to the world. In my name, men dispelled the forces of darkness, and joined forces with God and his angels. From my womb will be born a New Humanity, greater than Homo Sapiens, a Homo Bono worthy of God's Heaven.

I am Cristalle, the Goddess of Light, and I stand before you as your friend, your sister, your mother, your Goddess. I am the Greatness that was Egypt. I am the Glory that was Greece. I am the Grandeur that was Rome. I am the Wonder that was China.

For centuries past and for eons to come, I shall stand for order, law and clarity. I shall be a manner of thought, of love, of reason. Lifting their eyes towards me, philosophers shall discover the depths of thought and architects shall dream of the majesty of their palaces.

So come to me all you truth-seekers. Come to me, in my Assumption home, second only to my home on Mt. Olympus. Come to this consecrated rock – where truth, virtue and infinite beauty have mingled to give birth to the Consciousness of Man.

A yaya who stayed with the family for 58 years, rearing most of our children --- an old maid baptized Honorata Zaragosa, whom we rebaptized Horonata Zagarosa, and call "Ateng" --- was overheard giving advice to my eldest daughter Elvira nicknamed "Virus" because she is infectious and contagious in her advocacy of breastfeeding, and deadly to her adversaries in the milk industry. In the matter of choosing a husband, what Ateng said deserves to be preserved for future generations, and passed on to Cristalle on her wedding day.

Half the tears women shed in their lifetime, she said, are shed because of a husband's infidelity or plain jealousy. *"Ang mga babae talagang swapang sa lalake."* Do not therefore, she said, choose a man who is of the type other women will pursue all the time. Chose the one-woman man who will love only you.

The other half of a woman's tears, Ateng said, are shed about money. If you do not have enough of it so that you cannot enjoy security from hunger and the amenities of civilized living, then your marriage is doomed. On the other hand, if you have so much of it that you waste it in frivolity, that your husband throws it around to have a good time, well, your marriage is doomed too. So marry a man who can support you in the manner you are accustomed to, but who is not too rich that he will spoil you and your happiness.

One half of all the smiles women have in their lifetime, Ateng continued, are due to sunny memories nurtured and kept for a rainy day. So, store up some good times with the boyfriend; marry him with whom you share the happiest memories.

And the other half of a woman's smiles come from the knowledge that she has contributed much to the happiness of others, of her husband, her children, and if she has a heart big enough to love the rest of the world, then she is a thousand times blest. And remember, as the wise Wizard of Oz once said, "Ultimately it is not how much you love that matters, it is how much you are loved by others."

To end this talk, I offer to Cristalle and Justine, my version of the Irish toast. *May the golden sun crown your brow, and flowers bloom at your feet. May good fortune dog your heels, and fair winds be ever at your backs. And may you stay in heaven for a long time, before the devil finds out you've been gone.*

God bless you all. I thank you.
September 8, 2016

Part 13. Reminiscences of the Presidents of the Philippines

I was born in Manila on April 10, 1924. That makes me 92 years of age, old enough to meet and talk to every President that has ever been elected to lead our country. There were 16 of them all in all, one Emilio Aguinaldo of the First Republic, one Jose P. Laurel of the Japanese Puppet Republic, one Manuel L. Quezon of the Philippine Commonwealth and 13 from the Second Republic: Osmeña, Roxas, Quirino, Magsaysay, Garcia, Macapagal, Marcos, Cory Aquino, Ramos, Estrada, Arroyo, Pnoy Aquino, and Duterte. Count them, the lucky 13.

Before the First Republic in 1898, we were ruled by Spanish Governors-General; after the First Republic in 1902, we were ruled by American Governors-General, one of whom was Cameron Forbes, after whom Forbes Park was named, and whom I met when I was a student in MIT, the Massachusetts Institute of Technology, in 1948. Forbes was then 80 years of age, a patrician who lived with his sister in a suburb of Boston. I was his guest in the company of Rosie Osmeña and the Abad Santos sisters. He is an old bachelor which makes me suspect he is gay. His favorite possession is a souvenir from the Philippines, a piano made of solid narra that sounded like a guitar playing inside a closet, because the hardwood narra is not a good sounding board for a piano.

I met President Emilio Aguinaldo on July 21, 1940 at my grandfather's house together with President Manuel L. Quezon. My grandfather was an Assemblyman then, and both Quezon and Aguinaldo were his close friends, visiting him on his birthday, and reconciling after a bitter electoral fight in the 1935 elections when both ran for the presidency and Quezon won. ***

My most memorable moment with President Aguinaldo was in the 1960s when I was a member of President Diosdado Macapagal's cabinet as Chairman of the National Economic Council, when Anding Roces and I visited him to inform him that the Independence date was changed from July 4th to June 12th. He was already 92 years old, like I am now, and he was 29 years old when as President of the First Republic, he promulgated our Declaration of Independence. Aguinaldo is really the Father of our Country, as George Washington was Father of his. We owe Aguinaldo, our flag, our National Anthem, our first constitution and our first republic.

My most memorable moment with President Quezon was when my grandfather visited him in his private room in Malacañang, and he came out of the bathroom stark naked, as he usually does to show of his private parts, he is reputed to have he biggest penis in the Philippines. By God, it was really big.

I met President Sergio Osmena on the same date July 21, 1940 on the same occasion on my grandfather's birthday bash. He was not yet president, he was the Vice-President of Quezon.

I met President Jose P. Laurel when I came back from the USA in 1949 as the first Industrial Engineer of the country. He offered to make me the dean of the Commerce Department of the Lyceum of the Philippines.

After the War, in 1946, I went to the United States to study in the Massachusetts Institute of Technology (MIT), the foreign branch of Mapua. The first thing I did was to write a letter to Albert Einstein, asking to meet with him, with the realization that it was he who convinced President Franklin Delano Roosevelt to develop the Atom Bomb and end the war. Einstein called me up to tell me that he thought Filipinos only spoke Spanish, that he was surprised to receive a beautifully written letter in English from a Filipino. He then invited me to come and see him, and I did, my dean drove me to Princeton University himself. And there I met both Einstein and Robert Oppenheimer, the builder of the Atom Bomb. Both spoke of *Ahimsa*, to which they adhered, the love and respect for all living things. ###

I met President Manuel A. Roxas when he came to the National Foods Corporation where my father was General Manager, canning foods like adobo in the first factory of its type in the Philippines. The lady who was the factory superintendent was showing the President a cutting machine, when oops, she accidentally lost a finger. We brought her to the hospital completely forgetting about the missing finger. The next month the factory went bankrupt because nobody would buy its products, fearing that the missing finger will show up on the dinner plate.

I was a frequent guest in Malacañang during the incumbency of President Quirino, since my parents were also invited, and Tommy Quirino was my schoolmate and the boyfriend of my sister-in-law Helen, with whom he was dancing partner and the best dancer in the country.

I was appointed by President Ramon Magsaysay as member of the Board of National Steel and Shipyards Corporation and my best friend JV Cruz was appointed to his Cabinet as Press Secretary. I was instrumental in his election because I and JV discovered that Carlos Romulo, who was his political rival actually committed plagiarism of Adlai Stevenson, when he made his acceptance speech as the *Democrata* candidate, and had to withdraw his candidacy when exposed. I was also the childhood friend of Magsaysay's girl friend, Gloria V.

In 1958, I was selected to be an Eisenhower Fellow to stay study in the USA for a year. When I landed in the USA, I was invited to the White House by President Dwight D. Eisenhower himself, who had me for lunch and told me that as MacArthur's Aide before the War, he helped my grandfather Assemblyman Daniel Maramba, draft Commonwealth Act No. 1, The National Defense, and often slept over in the process.

After I came back, I became president of the United Crusade for Clean Elections (UNICRUCEL), when President Carlos P. Garcia ran for re-election against Diosdado Macapagal. Both were my good friends. Macapagal won, and he appointed me to his cabinet as Chairman of the National Economic Council. Senate President Ferdinand Marcos was part of my Council and he and I became good friends. I remember Marcos confiding to me that in the bathroom he shared with Imelda, there were two washbowls, one chest-high for Imelda, and one waist-high for Ferdie, because while Imelda uses hers to wash her face, he uses his to wash his private parts. Oh Ferdie, I told him, you are then a "washbowl ball washer." Hahaha. I dared not repeat that joke during martial law, I might have been castrated.

I was a partisan in favor of Cory Aquino in the Snap election of 1986, and participated in the Edsa Revolution that ousted Marcos after 14 years of Martial Law. I have so many stories about Martial Law, but my favorite was when my daughter Rosanna burst into our bedroom and shouted, "Marcos is gone, he fled to Hawaii." My wife Cecilia fell to her knees to thank the Lord, but my daughter, lifted her up and exclaimed, "No, no prayers, not yet. Heaven is empty. God and his angels are here dancing on the streets. Come let's join them."

Fidel V. Ramos was my childhood friend in Pangasinan. His father was the political protégé of my grandfather, my mother was his Godmother, and he in turn is the Godfather to my son Atom. His wife was my good friend when we were in the USA as students, she coming over to my dorms and typing my term papers. She complains, "When I finished typing his papers, Larry Henares would bring me home in a streetcar. Then in the evening he goes out with his American girlfriends in a taxi. And he claims to be a nationalist." And I answer, "Stop complaining, Ming the Merciless, you don't know what happens to the American girls inside the taxi."

Gloria Macapagal Arroyo is family to me, having known her since she was a little girl, having been a member of her father's cabinet, and having been a weekly guest at her house when her old man was still alive. I advised President Fidel Ramos, instead of endorsing Jose de Venecia as his successor, to endorse Gloria instead and run as her vice-president (or co-president). But he was too proud to do that. And Gloria ran as vice-president on her own. Think of it, if Gloria ran against Erap Estrada, she might have had a chance to beat him. But win or lose, the vice-president candidate Ramos was unbeatable, and would have succeeded Estrada when he was ousted in EDSA II. Think of it, Ramos would have served 9 years instead of 6, as President of the Philippines.

When Gloria in her turn announced that she may not run for election to succeed herself, she was applauded by the Filipino people, but I suggested that she runs for vice-president with Raul Roco as her President, knowing as a good friend that Roco was dying of cancer. Apparently she did not believe me, because she changed her mind and ran for the President, while Roco died just after elections. Think of it, if the Roco-Arroyo ticket won, Gloria might have been president and served for another six years, and still have been qualified to run again for another term of six years. Wow, she might have served a total of 15 years, Wow.

When Estrada was elected, I met him in an elevator. I greeted him, "Congratulations, Mr. President, how is Mrs., and Mrs., and Mrs. and Mrs. Estrada?" referring to his multiple wives, and he gamely answered, "They're fine, Larry, and fine, and fine and fine!"

I campaigned and voted for PNoy Aquino, but was a little disappointed in his style of governing. He appointed my daughter-in-law Kim Jacinto-Henares as Commissioner of the Bureau of internal Revenue, and sent 3 Senators to jail for plunder, but his cabinet officials were a disappointment, his bench was shallow, and he chose from his sister's friends, his classmates and shooting buddies. The many times my son and I were with him, he did all the talking and none of the listening. He ran a Student Council instead of a Presidency. He played TV games, drove fast cars, went on hot dates, went shooting –

which is what my boys did when they were 16. I don't think he ever grew up.

When the elections were nearing, I was asked as a journalist whom to vote for, and I answered, "It depends on you psychological make up. If you think the present is so perfect that any change is more likely for the worse than for the better, then vote for Mar Roxas and be assured that the if he is elected, the next six years will be exactly like the past six years. If you are a gambler like I am, or are 92 years old and cannot look forward to the next elections, if you want to make your last hurrah, then vote for Rodrigo Duterte, for change is coming, and you don't know whether we will spiral up to perfection or spiral down to perdition, but you are willing to take a chance. If you lost faith in your country, and really do not care if it goes down the drain, then vote for Jojo Binay who will steal you blind. Now if you want to change history, and court destiny, vote for Grace Poe, because if she wins, she will be the first American woman president in the history of the world, ahead of my *tocaya* Hillary Clinton!

Well, Digong Duterte won, and although he keeps us safe from drugs, corruption, and terrorism, we do not know what tomorrow will really bring. So let us postpone judgment and hope for the best.
October 25-27, 2016, UNTV

Part 14. Radical Islam by Fareed Zakaria
The next time you hear of a terror attack no matter where it is, no matter what the circumstances, you will likely think to yourself it's Muslims again and you will probably be right.

In 2014 about 30,000 people were killed in terror attacks worldwide. The vast majority of those perpetrating the violence were Muslims, but -- and this is important -- so were the victims. Of the 30,000 dead the vast, vast majority were Muslims. That's crucial to understand because it shed to light on the question, why do they hate us? Islamic terrorists don't just hate America or the west, they hate the modern world and they particularly hate Muslims who are trying to live in the modern world. Let's be clear, while the Jihadist are few, there is a larger cancer within the world of Islam, a cancer of backwardness and extremism and intolerance, most of the countries that have laws that restrict the laws of free exercise of religion on Muslim majority.

All that have lost against living the faith on Muslim majority. But are these things inherent in the religion? When experts tried to explain that in the 14th century Islamic civilization was the world most advanced, or that the Quran was once treated as a liberal and progressive document. They are not trying to deny the realities of backwardness today what they are saying is, it can change. Islam after all has been around for 14 centuries. There have been periods of war but also of peace. It's the same religion then and now, so what is different? It is not theology, it is politics. Radical Islam is the product of the broken politics and stagnant economics of Muslim countries. They have found in radical religion an ideology that lets them reign against the modern world. An ideology that is now being exported to alienated young Muslims everywhere in Europe and even in some rare cases in the United States.

So how to end this? There's really only one way, help the majority of Muslims fight extremists, reform their faith and modernize their societies. In doing so, we should listen to those on the front lines. Many of whom are fighting and dying in the struggle against Jihadist. The hundreds of Muslims reformers as I've spoken to say that their tasks is made much harder when Western politician and pundits condemn Islam entirely, demean their faith and speak of all Muslim as backward and suspect.

Here is another way to think about this. In America, Afro-Americans make up about 13 percent of the population, yet they comprise about 50 percent of homicide defenders according to a justice department study. Now we understand, I hope we understand that when we see a black man on the street we cannot, must not treat him as a likely criminal, it would be dehumanizing, unfair and racist. In America of all places people should be treated as individuals and not a stereotypes from a racial, ethnic or religious group. Remember, the Bangladeshi cab driver who drives you to the airport has nothing, nothing to do with ISIS even though he is also a Muslim.

It's hard not to make this quick associations especially in the wake of a terror attack. But if America is about anything it is the idea that people should be judged as individuals with individual liberties and rights. It is what they hate about us. We might as well live up to our own ideals.

This article neglects to say that Western corporations discovered oil in Arabian lands. The United States, Britain, France, and others supported dictatorships and monarchies, in order to get control of the oil. Radical Islam came about when Arabs had their popular leaders overthrown and replaced with corrupt rulers. One of the best known covert actions of the American Central Intelligence Agency (CIA) was its role in the 1953 overthrow of the Iranian government headed by Mohammed Mossadegh and the subsequent installation of the Shah Mohammad Reza Pahlavi into power. The Iranian Revolution of 1979 led to the overthrow of the Shah Dynasty and its eventual replacement with a National Republic under the Ayatollah Khomeini, the leader of the revolution, supported by leftist and Islamist organizations and Iranian student movements.
November 16, 2016

ooooo

RODRIGO DUTERTE

Part 1. Duterte's Background

Rodrigo Roa Duterte was born on March 28, 1945 at Maasin, Southern Leyte to Vicente G. Duterte, who served as Governor of Davao and Soledad Roa, a school teacher and a civic leader.He spent his elementary days at the Sta. Ana Elementary School in Davao City, where he graduated in 1956. He finished his secondary education at the Holy Cross of Digos after spending s fee years at the Ateneo de Davao. For his tertiary education, he took up a Bachelor of Arts degree at the Lyceum of the Philippines University, where he graduated in 1968. He also obtained a law degree from San Beda College in 1972. In the same year, he passed the bar exam. He served as prosecutor in Davao City for over a decade.

After the 1986 People Power Revolution, Duterte was appointed officer – in – charge vice mayor. In 1988, he ran for mayor and won, serving until 1998. He set a precedent by designating deputy mayors that represented the Lumad and Moro in the city government, which was later copied in other parts of the country. In 1998, because he was term – limited to run again for mayor, he ran for the House of Representatives and won as Congressman of the 1st District of Davao City. In 2001, he ran again for mayor in Davao and was again elected for his fourth term. He was reelected in 2004 and in 2007. In 2010, he was elected vice mayor, succeeding his daughter, Sara Duterte – Carpio, who was elected as mayor.

Governance Innovations

Established one of the first Local Government Investment Promotion Programs in the early 90s, now the Davao City Investment Promotion Center, and promoted relations with counterpart local governments in the Brunei Indonesia Malaysia Philippines Growth Corridor.

Through the support of Duterte, the City Council amended the ordinance no. 1627, Series of 1994, which imposed a prohibition on selling, serving, drinking and consumption of liquors and alcoholic beverages from 1:00 am until 8:00 am.

Organized Task Force Davao with police and military that has become a model for other LGUs

Davao also successfully implemented a smoking ban in

public places.

Executive Order no. 39 was signed by Duterte, setting the speed limits for all kinds of motor vehicles within the territorial jurisdiction of Davao City in the interest of public safety and order.

The City Government of Davao established the central 911 emergency management system and Public Safety Command Center.

Mayor Rodrigo Duterte, through E.O no. 24, ordered all shopping malls and commercial centers to install, operate and maintain high end and high definition closed circuit television (CCTV) cameras in all entrance and exit points of their premises.

Davao City sent rescue and medical teams to Tacloban to give aid to the victims of Typhoon Haiyan (Yolanda). Financial assistance was also given to Bohol and Cebu for the earthquake victims.

Women And Children

Established a gender sensitive crisis intervention unit, programs dealing Violence against Women and children, providing free legal and temporary shelter assistance, a child minding center and promulgated an antidiscrimination ordinance outlawing discrimination based on gender ethnicity and religion.

Awards

Davao City under Duterte won the National Literacy Hall of Fame Award for being a three – time first place winner in the Outstanding Local Government Unit Highly Urbanized City category.

Davao City under his watch, was recently awarded most child friendly city in 2014, one of the Health Champions awarded by DOH and Jesse Robredo Foundation and a Gender and Development E-Learning Hub by the Philippine Commission on women in 2015, and the DILG seal of good governance in August 2015. These are but the latest among numerous awards and citations received since the 1990s.

Part 2. Platform of Rodrigo Duterte, draft by Henares

I SHALL RESPECT, DEFEND AND OBEY THE CONSTITUTION OF THE PHILIPPINES TO THE BEST OF MY ABILITY, SO HELP ME GOD.

If it is the will of God that I am elected by the people as the President of the Philippines, I swear upon my honor, and this is no empty political promise to court your votes, to pursue the following platform, come rain or shine, no ifs no buts. And if you do not believe me, or have doubts that I would not or cannot do it, or if you do not agree with some of the things I want to do, please do not vote for me.

Crime, Peace and Order

First, I shall order ALL guns confiscated, unlicensed or in the possession of political goons or private armies. No one shall be allowed to have more than one firearm, except gun collectors whose extra guns shall have their firing pins deactivated, and except legitimate and duly licensed security agencies.

Second, I shall order that no motorcycle be allowed to carry two grown men in tandem, to prevent assassinations and various crimes that have been proliferating recently. We shall ease this restriction when such crimes are reduced to a manageable level.

Third, I shall have a law passed to increase the penalty for, and have absolute Zero Tolerance for drug pushers. druglords, rapists, murderers, any policemen or soldier who kill or kidnap anyone they are supposed to protect, and prison officials who release prisoners to do murder-for-hire. Let us not delude ourselves that our prisons rehabilitate, more often they serve as schools for the furtherance of crime. I shall reduce the prison population by actual prevention of crime.

Fourth, any prison official allowing prisoners to store weapons and drugs will be summarily fired and put to jail, and his immediate superior fired immediately, and I don't care if he is a friend, classmate, or shooting buddy.

Fifth, I will issue an Executive Order, pursuing a policy of Affirmative Action for our Muslim brothers, tribal minorities, women, including LGBT – much like what Presidents Kennedy and Johnson did for the African-Americans to jumpstart the Civil Rights Movement -- urging business firms doing business with the national government, government entities and state schools to offer job opportunities and scholarships to minorities, specially the Muslims, to the extent of their percentage share of total population of the Philippines, in order to integrate them into the body politic. This way, we may wean the Muslims away from their feudal lords who have ruled them like warlords, and kept them poor and powerless and subject to cultural shock every time they encounter their Christian brothers.

Sixth, in the interest of justice, I shall order all fiscals to initiate court proceedings against anyone lying under oath. There is an epidemic of lying and liars in this country, and I know of no one ever convicted of perjury in our courts. After every high profile case, we shall go after every witness known to have lied under oath and put him to jail.

Traffic Congestion

As a general rule, we must change our mindset and priorities. Railroads and mass transit are primary; highways, streets and roads secondary. In crowded cities, bicycles, rail transits, buses and transport of goods are primary; private cars and motorcycles are secondary. In rich progressive cities like New York, even the rich take the subways.

First, we shall give priority in street lanes to ambulances, police cars, buses, and trucks transporting goods, and specially to bicycles and non-motorized tricycles, and relegate private cars, and specially cars of government officials to a few lanes. No wang-wang is to be allowed except for the President of the Philippines.

Second, the rehabilitation and immediate extension of LRT, MRT, and Philippine National Railroads are to be prioritized over streets and highways.

Third, we shall allow the importation of secondhand cars guaranteed to last five years more, and no longer license cars older than 12 years, other than those for collection of old and classic cars.

Fourth, we will decongest Metro Manila and solve the squatter problem by the Van-GO method, manufacturing housing units with 40-foot container vans for squatters, stack them up to 5 stories, occupying 1/5 of the space of the squatter area, relocating and housing the squatters ON THE SAME DAY we destroy their shanties. These Van-GO units can be transported readily to NewTowns elsewhere as soon as railroads and highways make these feasible.

Creating Jobs, Our Economy.

As a general rule, I believe with the priests and religious orders, the kibutzims and enlightened socialists, that the nation must demand, receive and give "from each according to his talents, and to each according to his needs." I believe fervently in the market economy, the ability of market forces to dictate business decisions. The basic economic forces are Capital and Labor; and I feel that it is unjust to allow Capital to flow freely across national borders while the migration of Labor is restricted, allowing Capitalist countries a high living standard at our expense. Industrialized countries are rich, agricultural countries are poor; and industrialized countries have the most productive agriculture. I pledge to industrialize our country.

First, without violating international obligations, I shall endeavor to encourage basic industries processing raw materials (like iron ore into ingots), then secondary industries to convert raw materials to industrial materials (like ingots to sheets and bars), and finally tertiary industries to convert the material to commercial products (like sheets to galvanized roofing). I shall do these, by tax-exemption, long term industrial loans, cheap land, and all means available to allow them to meet foreign competition.

Second, I shall demand legislation (a) to restore the basic right of employers to hire and fire employees, without government intervention, except under the provisions of a collective agreement, (b) to discourage self-defeating strikes and demonstrations, in favor of compulsory arbitration. (c) to discourage commercial firms violating the spirit of our laws, by marathon use of temporary contract workers instead of giving them the rights and benefits that permanent workers are entitled to.

Third, I believe the Agrarian Reform that we have been pursuing is an utter failure; it has impoverished the landowning class without improving the lot of the tenants who are forced to go back to a carabao economy. I shall suspend any transfer of lands without adequate compensation to the land owners based on the real market value of the land. I shall introduce legislation following the pattern started by Japanese Emperor Meiji, when he bought the lands of the landowning class at prices higher than market, PROVIDED the landowners invest the money in industries, thus creating the Zaibatsu class of industrialists. Thus did the Emperor transform his country from an agricultural country to an industrialized one – from 1864 to 1900, a mere 36 years.

Fourth, it is a shame that in a country where all you have to do is to flick a seed into the ground to make it grow, we cannot even grow enough rice to feed ourselves. No more shall we import rice to subsidize consumption. We shall instead subsidize the farmer with an Agricultural Price Support and Stabilization Program. We shall set a price that will give the farmer a fair return for his efforts, buy rice at that price when the market price is too low, and sell the rice when the price is too high, while setting up rice storage granaries for emergencies. We shall promote the mechanization of agriculture, and new technology and industrialization to reduce unemployment.

Fifth, it is a shame that in country when most of our workers are unemployed, we do not have enough houses to live in, goods to consume, not enough schools, libraries, museums and theaters to edify our people. The economic value of an idle day is lost forever. Let us follow the example of China which developed its economy by employing its huge army of unemployed to produce for itself and a huge market of consumers. In this connection, instead of spending our money on conditional cash transfers to promote mendicancy, instead of supporting our crooked politicians by pork barrel, ghost payrolls, and other forms of graft, instead of supporting a vast network of useless bureaucrats, let us do what Franklin Delano Roosevelt did during the American depression, create an NRA (National Recovery Administration) to create work, building dams, railroads, subways, and other necessary infrastructures.

Sixth, I believe that free easy access to the Internet and the Social Media is a basic human right, and I cannot countenance a monopoly allowed by the National Telecommunications Commission to charge 12 times the cost for 1/10th the internet speed than those enjoyed by netizens of Singapore and South Korea; to allow one firm to monopolize the Internet Exchanges (IX) without insisting on Internet Peering as HongKong and Singapore does.

Education

First, I believe that it is the moral obligation of the government to provide the best education possible to its citizens. I believe that the K to 12 system now in place, deserves to be implemented fully in conjunction with the participation of the Department of Education for all public sand private schools, the CHED for universities and higher education, and TESDA for vocational schools.

Second, we must ensure that enough classrooms, even if on a makeshift basis, are built to accommodate all who want to study, and encourage the enrollment of more teachers to man all these classrooms.

Third, make it easier to organize tax free Foundations to fund scholarships for education of qualified students like Foundation of Philippine Business for Social Progress.

Fourth, encourage the establishment of more innovative approaches to good education, and more schools of the traditional kind, by tax incentives.

Moral Regeneration

While I believe that it is no business of government to intervene or judge what its citizens think, or do with their bodies in the privacy of their homes, as long as they do not harm anyone else, I believe that the government is obligated to promote moral values and a code of ethics that will govern their public life and relationships among each other as civilized human beings, through its schools, NGOs and religious organization – knowing that this moral regeneration can only be effective, when accompanied by economic measures to achieve full employment and satisfaction of the citizens' most basic needs:

First, I shall create a Presidential Task Force for Values Formation, among the leaders of selected religious organizations, schools and NGOs, to formulate this Code of Ethics, and to exert their influence to denounce and correct the unethical behavior of our politicians, bureaucrats and businessmen. I shall use the ubiquitous cell-phone and social media in the hands of the citizenry to monitor compliance.

Second, I shall exorcize the hypocrisy of so-called religious leaders, by investigating all such leaders, including priests and bishops, for fornicating, for hiding families born in sin, and for sexually abusing children; and expose them to public ridicule.

Third, I will ask for legislation for the full implementation of the Constitutional provision against Political Dynasties, even if my own running mate and another presidential candidate are neck-deep in their involvement. And if Congress refuses, I shall lead a People's Referendum directing that anyone related to an elected official within 6 degrees of consanguinity, cannot run in an election for any public office, unless otherwise provided by law.

Foreign Policy

First, I will declare that we Filipinos shall no longer be slavish to the interest of another country at the expense of our own, shall never again be inveigled to enter into unequal treaties and will develop free and unaligned relations with all nations;

Second, while we shall honor the EDCA, the VFA and other treaties with the USA, for mutual interest and benefit, and continue to oppose Chinese incursions into our territory, we shall reach out to our brothers in the ASEAN and in Asia.

Third, we shall continue to pursue our claim to Sabah which the British stole from us.

Fourth, we shall perform all the duties and obligations of our membership in the United Nations and all its Agencies, specially the WHO/UNICEF, especially if it concerns the health of the citizens, and measures to counteract climate change.

Health

First, we support the United Nations in controlling the spread of contagious and communicable diseases, like Zika, Bird Flu, MERS, Nipha Virus that threaten humans constantly on the move.

Second, we support the availability of vaccines for such diseases as influenza and dengue fever, tuberculosis, malaria and others endemic to the Philippines..

Third, we should expand the Generics movement to ensure cheaper medicines for the masses.

Fourth, we should increase the number of health clinics to cover all barangays, and encourage the enrollment of doctors, nurses, med-techs and paramedics, to man these clinics, to help decongest hospitals.

Fifth, expand the facilities of nutritional activities to cover school lunches, day care centers, and health clinics.

Sixth, we shall religiously pursue the declared Millennium Development Goals of the WHO, specially those involving infant morbidity, infant and mother mortality, and specifically the WHO/UNICEF Declaration on the Marketing of Milk and others, supporting Breastfeeding against Bottlefeeding as the Norm in the nurturing of the human race.

Seventh, we hail the efforts on the national and local levels to give special attention to the needs and well-being of our senior citizens, a movement of which the Philippines have been pioneers and innovators.

Eighth, we hail the existence of safety nets for our population, the SSS for the general public and GSIS for government employees, and specially the universal health insurance extended by the PhilHealth under Alexander Padilla, its CEO.

Environment and Climate Change

For the first time in 20 years, a binding universal agreement on climate change is made possible by the 2015 UN Climate Change Conference convening in Paris upon the initiative of France and countries most impacted by natural disasters, such as the Philippines. The key roles are played by the United States and China, the two largest emitters of greenhouse gases. On December 12, 2015, 195 countries agreed to reduce carbon emissions and keep global warming "to well below 2 degrees Celsius, to prevent the melting of ice caps that would cause the raising of ocean levels that threaten our coastal areas.

As a country prone to natural disasters, we responded with our own agenda:

First, we should encourage setting up alternative sources of clean energy, like Solar Energy as in Negros, wind power as in the Ilocos, making use of free government land not devoted to agriculture, along with tax incentives..

Second, we should continue developing waterfalls and geothermal sources for the generation of power.

Third, we have explored the possibility of generating methane gas from animal waste, and the use of coconut oil as a substitute for diesel fuel; as well as alcohol as an additive to gasoline.

Fourth, we won a Guinness World Record for the planting the most trees, along the entire National Highway. We should encourage planting more forest cover in remote areas.

Fifth, despite many obstacles we have managed to keep alive our most threatened wildlife: Philippine Monkey eating eagle, Tarsius monkey, Philippine Tamaraw.

Sixth, our Clean Air Act and legislation on mining and business, have kept our air, water, and soil relatively free from pollutants.

Seventh, we have managed to keep our reputation for having the most biological diversity in flora and fauna in the world.

Disaster Response

We should learn from the mistakes we made during the disaster of Typhoon Yolanda, to wit:

First and foremost is that there should be NO involvement of politics in disaster response.

Second, there should be no bureaucratic impediment to the flow of relief goods to those in need; there should be a law that exempts donated goods from duties and taxes, and a mechanism that prevents diversion of such goods to the black market.

Third, there are two most essential requirements in a disaster, food and shelter – there should already be canned foods, tents and recycled housing units in storage for the emergency, as well as manufacturing facilities to speedily make additional pre-fabricated housing units. Such temporary shelters should be used and re-stored and recycled for the next emergency.

Fourth, there should be a well-coordinated volunteer task force to assemble relief goods and cash that are being donated from all parts of the Philippines and abroad, in units ready to be delivered to affected families.

Fifth, and most important, the disaster response should be headed by one well-known for his honesty and trustworthiness, for his initiative, innovation and talent for organization, preferably from the business sector.

Corruption

The real engine of growth and development is not government but Business and private initiative. It marshals money, machines and materials and provides goods for the consumers, jobs for the unemployed, profits for the investors, and tax income for the government. Corruption in its most virulent form is government that impedes the honest and efficient practice of business. And such corruption infests all levels of government. Who is to blame, and who can do the most to prevent corruption? "The buck stops here," said President Harry Truman. The leader is the crux, leadership is of the essence. We have to elect a president who is absolutely honest and trustworthy, strict and straight, with a passion for transparency and public accountability.

First, he has to select the best and the brightest among the DOERS, pay them well, tell them what he expects them to achieve, and give them a DEADLINE for the performance of their jobs.

Second, at the first instance they do not perform, he gives them a warning; the next time he fires them without hesitancy. Once he does this, the entire bureaucracy will toe the line.

Third, he demands absolute honesty, integrity and transparency, no ifs, no buts, and anyone who does not look and smell clean is summarily fired.

Fourth, the leader must emphasize and make the people believe, that the duty of government is to allocate resources to ensure that all citizens are rendered Justice above all, protected against the extremes of poverty, educated, edified and developed to the best they can be.

Fifth, we were able to indict three senators and their collaborators incarcerated for plunder, and forbid a high profile city mayor from ever seeking public office. The so-called *Daan Matuwid* policy that accomplished this, has been accused of selective justice, but indications are, except with the possibility that one particular corrupt candidate will get elected Peresident, this public policy will most probably survive in future administrations.

Part 3. What is the problem?

What is the problem about choosing a president among those who are currently nominated in the present presidential election? Time was when a journalist lays down his choices by delineating the differences between good, better and best; nowadays, in the Philippines as well as in the United States, one is left with the choice between bad, worse and worst.

I am about to write a piece of satire, which many of our readers rarely understand or appreciate. Filipinos usually feel that I am embarking on a barrage of insults, but it is far from the truth. The role of satire is to ridicule or criticize those attitudes and vices in society, which the writer considers a threat to civility and rational discourse. The function of satire is not to make others laugh at persons or ideas the writer makes fun of. It intends to warn the public and to change their opinions about the prevailing attitudes and conditions in society. Satire and irony are interlinked. Irony is the difference between what is said or done and what is actually meant. Therefore, writers frequently employ satire and irony to point at the dishonesty and silliness of individuals and society and criticize them by ridiculing them.

I was telling an old friend of mine how confused I was in selecting the presidential candidate I'd vote for. My friend who is wise in political matters, laughed and posited, "What's the problem? It depends on your psyche," he said, "If you feel that the present is so perfect, that any change is more likely for the worse than for the better, then you vote for MAR ROXAS, and be content that the next six years would be exactly the same as the last six years. If you are a gambler who believes in the throw of the dice, and takes a chance that either the Philippines would spiral up to perfection, or spiral down to perdition, then vote for RODRIGO DUTERTE, and leave your country to the Fates. Now, if you feel that the Philippines is hopeless and deserves to go down the drain, vote for JEJOMAR BINAY. Ah, but if you want to change history and court destiny, vote for GRACE POE, and if she wins, you will have elected the first American female president in history, 7 months before Hillary Clinton assumes office. And you may have nudged our Philippines into being the 51st State of the American Union, the ultimate dream of every Little Brown Brother with a colonial mentality."

Don't laugh, he said seriously, no Filipino president ever assumed office who did not promote the interest of Mother America above that of the Philippines. It is wonderful to be part of the American nation. We will have added our 100 million population to America's 325 million people, and increase its population by a full third. More than a century and a half ago, when Texas was admitted to the Union, it was given the option, due to its size, to divide itself into 5 states; and if we decide to exercise the same option, we will be entitled to 10 senators out of 60, and 134 representatives out of a total of 569 – we will at the outset be the greatest political constituency in the country, bigger than the Afro-Americans and the Latinos combined – and with our sex appeal, libido and propensity to multiply, we can make half-breeds out of the red-necks and white trash in short order, and shatter the myth of racial superiority forever.

And to punish America for it did to the Afro-Americans (slavery), the Indians (genocide) and the Filipinos (zona, water cure, economic exploitation and Balanginga Massacre), we could elect Binay and BongBong to the presidency of the United States, and amend its constitution to change its name to the United States of the Philippines.

April 18, 2016

Part 4.   Losing Grace, by Inquirer Editorial, comment by Henares

Almost five years after the crime, security guard Lester Ivan Rivera was meted out three life terms for the rape-slay of 19-year-old computer science student Given Grace Cebanico in October 2011.

The crime had shocked not only the UP Los Baños community but also all parents nationwide. Given Grace's bruised body was found in a canal near the campus by a morning jogger. She had been shot in the forehead and stabbed several times; her mouth was stuffed with cloth, her hands tied behind her. For two days before then, her parents had been frantically searching for her.

No one deserves such a brutal death, least of all this young woman who had literally been God's gift of grace to her parents, thus her name—a name that also reflected her character, as a video of her singing and hosting a Sunday school event showed. A cheerful soul, a diligent student and a good daughter was how her father Daniel, a pastor, described her.

As her parents would learn, Given Grace stayed out late on that fateful night to finish a school project in a classmate's dorm, and was on her way back to her own dorm on campus when accosted and forced into a tricycle driven by one Percival de Guzman. He and security guard Rivera had planned "only" to rob Given Grace, as had been their wont with other UPLB students every time they needed cash after a gambling loss. But she was so pretty, Rivera confessed later, after his grandfather got wind of the crime and surrendered him to authorities.

Rivera and De Guzman punched Given Grace until she lost consciousness, and took turns raping her, police said. A third man, who jumped off the tricycle when he realized what the two others had in mind, positively identified them. Police recovered from them an iPhone which, when switched on, had Given Grace's picture as wallpaper. De Guzman awaits sentencing next month.

Yet even justice served will not stem the grief of Given Grace's parents. We miss her so much, Daniel Cebanico said. "I wish we could again hold her in our arms and tell her we love her very much."

Nor will Rivera's sentence quell the anxiety among parents of students at UPLB, the scene of a number of rape-slays, such as that of 14-year-old sampaguita vendor Rochel Geronda only a few months after Given Grace's own ordeal. This forested campus first hit the headlines in 1993 with the gang rape and murder of student Eileen Sarmenta by a cabal led by then Calauan Mayor Antonio Sanchez, who are all serving seven life terms. That case should have immediately prompted a serious evaluation of security measures given the vastness of the area and the diverse population of its neighboring barangays.

But time and again, after the hue and cry have settled down, things revert back to pretty much what they were. And one is prompted to ask: Are our girls so expendable that authorities can't—or won't—do more for them? The evening news is littered with stories of little girls gone missing and later found dead—in grassy lots, abandoned buildings or waterways, abused by strangers and even neighbors who had likely offered them a sweet treat.

And what of parents who direct their children to strip and simulate sex acts before a video camera, their images then sold on the internet to pedophiles and perverts worldwide? The rationalization is that they're only pictures, and the children weren't touched, as if being peddled onscreen weren't in fact abuse and a glaring cause for concern.

But these are exceptions, it's been said, out of the norm so they become news. We're a matriarchal society, it's been pointed out, we've had two women presidents, hundreds of women officials, some of the world's most influential businesswomen, international beauty queens, and one of the highest literacy rates for women.

And, it's been bragged about, we're not as bad as China, where a one-child policy meant couples disposing of infant girls to be able to try again for the preferred male heir. Or Nigeria, where Islamist militants kidnap little girls and treat them as sex slaves, sell them off in marriage, or turn them into suicide bombers.

Well, no. But every day we lose grace. We have a presidential contender who treats rape as a joke and won't apologize for it. He remains acceptable—and actually enjoys wide, even delighted, support for all his misogynist views. It's very telling of how women and girls are regarded in this proudly Christian nation. End of editorial.

This is Larry Henares contributing a few cents worth of comments to this Inquirer editorial. First of all it is not true that the presidential contender who treated rape as a joke, did not apologize for it; he did so after a fashion, but was not forgiven by most people who were scandalized by it. It was not "his misogynist views" that that got him acceptance and "wide, even delighted support" from the electorate and got him elected as President of the Philippines. It was his carefully cultivated reputation for being hard on criminals, especially rapists, drug pushers and murderers that endeared him to the voters ahead of all the other candidates who are perceived to be traditional politicians (trapos), spineless and inutile. Apparently the voters did not mind Duterte's bad jokes and foul mouth, as long as he can keep our women safe from rapists and our citizens free of criminals operating with impunity.

Secondly, I believe that Duterte is right in telling the Australian and American Ambassadors to "shut up and stop interfering with our domestic affairs," knowing that for a long time Australian low-types have been setting up seedy bars in the Philippines, where Filipinas are offered as door prizes and for auctions; that Australian tourists, bored with buggering sheep, come to the Philippines sex tourists and pedophiles; that Australian husbands murder their Filipina wives six times more frequently than they kill their Australian wives; that Australian whites descended from criminals exiled from London, and who subsequently committed genocide on the dark aborigines and the dodo birds. Also, Duterte was told that Ambassador Philip Goldberg is from the intelligence (that is spying) community of the State Department and who as Ambassador to Bolivia, was thrown out of the country for financing the opposition and interfering in domestic affairs; he is also rumored to have visited the Iglesia ni Cristo to threaten them with a tax case in the USA if they support Duterte's candidacy. Duterte does not like him.

Secondly I have changed a lot from my days as a "bleeding heart" against the death penalty and concerned about the rehabilitation of criminals. I believe in Justice; Love you have to earn; mercy you have to beg for; but Justice, you can demand as a matter of right! Fiat justitia, ruat coelum! Let Justice be done, though the heavens fall! Upon this principle Rome built a civilization that lasted for a thousand years.

I believe that victims are more entitled to justice than criminals are. They deserve the "blood money" for restitution. Prisons do not rehabilitate, they are schools that teach criminals to be worse criminals. Why should we waste public money on the recidivists?   Restore the death penalty for grave crimes. Restore penalties that fit the crime: hanging, beheading, electrocution, garroting, firing squad, lethal injection.   Let criminals suffer the pain they inflict on their victims. Bury the criminals where their remains enrich the soil for agriculture. Solve overpopulation.
May 19-20, 2016, UNTV

Part 5. Election 2016

Today is the Time of Decision, the Moment of Truth. Many unusual, unexpected and extraneous events will influence the results of our elections: the impeachment and expulsion of Chief Justice Renato Corona, Hospital Arrest of President Gloria M. Arroyo; the appointment of Conchita Morales Carpio as Ombudsman, of Chief Justice Lourdes Serreno at the age of 53; the Janet Napoles plunder case; the incarceration of Senators Juan Ponce Enrile, Jinggoy Estrada, and Bong Estrada; the dismissal of Makati Mayor Junjun Binay; Mamasapano Massacre; suspension of PNP chief Alan Purissima; the devastating Yolanda Typhoon, the strongest to hit the planet.

The Daan Matuwid policy of President PNoy was overshadowed by the Supreme Court ruling against the Disbursement Acceleration Fund, charges of graft inefficiency and corruption against those in charge of the Metro Rail Transit, and "selective justice" against crooked officials.

There are five candidates for the Presidency, in the order of survey popularity: Rodrigo Duterte (accused womanizing and extrajudicial killing of criminals), Grace Poe (whose status as a natural-born Filipino is still subject to judicial review); Jejomar Biinay who is being accused of massive graft and corruption; Mar Roxas, known for ineptness, elitism and analysis-paralysis; and feisty Miriam Defensor Santiago, afflicted with Stage-4 cancer. Two candidates want to bury the dictator Marcos in the Libingan ng mga Bayani; one wants to concede the disputed islands to China for a railroad network; at least two of them would appoint Iglesia ni Cristo members to the Supreme Court; another two would leave the judicial appointees to the approval of The Firm and Opus Dei.

It is time for us Filipinos to realize that the future of our country depends on the resolution of national issues, a redefinition of national purposes, a vision of national destiny. If we persist in being distracted by things that do not really matter or are bad for us in the long run, if we allow our political decisions to be diverted to matters of irrelevance or of outright criminal intent, then we are doomed as a nation.

We must remind our people that the art of politics, according to Emmet John Hughes, is not to mend the petty conflicts of the moment, nor to close some tiny gap in the discourse of the day. The art of politics is to define and to advance designs and policies for a thousand tomorrows.

A thousand tomorrows hence, may it not be said that our politicians have squandered their energies in petty conflicts and daily discourse, and failed at the most crucial time of our history to set the stage for the fulfillment of our people's aspirations ---- that in the blindness of their intramural squabbles they have shunted the course of industrialization, dimmed the cause of nationalism, and doomed to abortion the birth of our nation.

May it rather be said that our politicians, regardless of party or personality, under the inspired leadership of our duly elected leaders, did unite in common cause for the common good, that our nation may survive and prosper for a thousand tomorrows till the end of time. Enough said. Go out and vote wisely and intelligently.

This day will slowly roll by, the hours toll, the minutes tick, as we the people of this country --- the waving, cursing, cheering millions of the electorate --- troop one by one, into the voting booth. There quietly and alone --- in that instant of sublime solitude when we are so utterly sovereign --- we will render our final decision.

Till then, the history of the next 6 years, and probably the next hundred years --- will stand, waiting, poised and ready --- waiting to be suddenly launched and set upon its course.
May 9, 2016, UNTV

Part 6. Duterte is not the Donald Trump of the Philippines

The foreign press has called our elected President, "Do-Dirty Harry" recalling the movie character of Clint Eastwood, and "Donald Trump of the Philippines," with reference to his "vigilante reputation," his foul mouth and womanizing. The similarity ends there, there is a world of difference between Duterte and Trump, and a world of similarities between Duterte and the other candidate that has captured the fascination of American Democrats: Senator Bernie Sanders. Sanders and Duterte are poor self-proclaimed Socialists; billionaire Trump is a boastful capitalist. Sanders and Duterte take the most liberal views, left of center: higher minimum wage for the working man, women's right of choice on planned parenthood contrary to the stand of the Catholic Church, support for gay and minority rights, opposition to the political influence of the wealthy, advocates of clean energy and environmental protection. Trump is a bigot, a right of center conservative against immigration of Latinos and Muslim refugees, non-believer of climate change, and advocate of coal and fossil fuel, contemptuous of women, a gun-nut and a war-monger. Our Rodrigo Duterte is not the Donald Trump of the Philippines. Rather, it may be said that Bernie Sanders is the Rodrigo Duterte of the United States.

Senator Bernie Sanders is a socialist who dared to bring out the success story of Scandinavian "Christian" socialism, particularly that of Sweden, to challenge the "exceptionalist view" of both Democrats and Republicans that the "United States is the greatest country on earth, period." He is given no chance to win the Democratic nomination, or the general election. Donald Trump is being touted as a potential winner against Democrat Hillary Clinton, at least by the Fox News. On the other hand, Mayor Rodrigo Duterte did Sanders one better. He told the US Ambassador Philip Goldberg to shut up and stop interfering in our internal affairs, as he was accused of doing in Bolivia in his last post. He handily won the Philippine election winning 38.65 % of the votes cast by voters who comprised 81% of the electorate – a record turnout dwarfing whatever US voters had ever done. He offered to grant amnesty to political prisoners, invited the head of the Communist Party to come home from his exile in Netherlands, and actually offered Communists to four posts in his cabinet: Labor, Agrarian Reform, Environment and Social Welfare. Then he told President Obama that he intends to conduct bilateral talks with China, potentially upsetting the US power shift to the Pacific Ocean.

Fox News states that "Socialism destroys democracy" in an effort to denigrate the Sanders Democratic wing, by citing Venezuela and Cuba. But Sweden is a different and untold story, a Third Way between Socialist Welfare State and market-oriented Capitalism, with free medical care coverage for all from cradle to grave; free tuition for university students; guaranteed free housing for all; subsidized childcare; paid parental leave (13 months leave at 80 percent pay); extensive unemployment benefits (including cash transfers as well as job training and retraining programs); generous pensions; provision for the disabled; and care for the elderly, full employment (2% unemployment vs. 5.5% in the USA; poverty rates very low compared to the USA; low income and wealth inequality lower than the USA; one of the lowest infant mortality rates. By contrast, the U.S. has the third most unequal wealth distribution and has the third highest rate of infant mortality. So which is the better country? Sweden, of course, not the USA.
June 6, 2016

Part 7. Duopoly, from an Inquirer Editorial, comments by Henares

Change is coming. But apparently not in the telecommunications sector where public complaints continue to mount against the high cost of internet service, which is so bad that it ranks among the world's slowest. Consumers had been awaiting the launch of a third telco player by diversified conglomerate San Miguel Corp. since last year. Hopes ran high when SMC chief executive Ramon Ang announced a possible joint venture with Telstra Corp. Ltd., Australia's biggest telco.

But last week came the news: SMC sold its Vega Telecom Inc. to the PLDT-Globe duopoly for P69.1 billion. Vega is the holding company of SMC's telco assets, including Eastern Telecoms, Liberty Telecoms, BellTel and Extelcom. PLDT and Globe's apparent target was SMC's valuable radio frequencies, particularly the 700 megahertz spectrum, which is capable of covering a wide area at a much lower cost.

The entry of a third telco would have resulted in real competition among the service providers, unlike the current duopoly where one firm only has to follow what the other is doing. Competition is proven to benefit consumers. Such was the case in 2003-2011 when the Gokongwei group's Digitel launched Sun Cellular. It disrupted the market duopoly by offering unlimited 24/7 voice calls and SMS for P250 a month and lowered the cost of international calls, such that it breached the 1-million-subscriber mark after only a year of operation.

Smart and Globe filed a complaint at the National Telecommunications Commission about Sun Cellular's alleged predatory and discriminatory pricing, but the NTC dismissed this. To finally stamp out the competition, in 2011 PLDT acquired the Gokongwei family's Digital Telecommunications Philippines Inc. in a P74-billion swap deal. While PLDT promised the NTC that it would continue operating Sun Cellular, nobody hears anything about it anymore. For all intents and purposes, Sun Cellular is gone and the duopolistic monopoly is back.

This time around, PLDT and Globe launched a massive PR campaign seeking to get part of the coveted 700 MHz spectrum owned by SMC. They threatened a court suit in order to force a redistribution of the frequency. This was a major factor in Telstra's decision last March to back out of the planned joint venture with SMC.

To avert potential public backlash from the deal, PLDT and Globe have promised that the newly bought assets would translate to faster mobile internet services as early as before

Christmas, but they gave no assurance that prices would be lowered. Globe's CEO was more to the point. Even with the added frequencies, he said, consumers should not expect prices to dip soon. He said mobile browsing rates here are already at par with the region and prices could go down in the near-term only if the incoming administration would assist in removing certain fees imposed by local government units, like so-called tower fees and social acceptability fees.

To soften possible regulatory action against the deal, PLDT and Globe have also promised to return some of the acquired frequencies to the government, enough for a third player to come in. But Globe's president believes otherwise. Even as other markets need competition, he said, keeping the telecommunications sector "healthy" means that two players are enough. The Philippines, he went on, is different from other markets given its combination of huge capital spending, bureaucratic red tape in dealing with LGUs, and the need to maintain profit margins, all while consumers demand lower prices.

The public can now rely on only two possible things. One is for the incoming administration to appoint as NTC head someone who has the consumers' welfare foremost in heart and mind. The other is for the newly minted Philippine Competition Commission to look objectively at the deal and see if consumers will truly benefit from it through improved service at a lower cost. SMC's feasibility study has shown that it can be done. As for PLDT and Globe, which appear to have bullied a potential third player and game-changer into giving up, we can only wait if their promise of faster mobile internet service will happen. We cannot, of course, expect it to be cheaper. The duopoly did not spend nearly P70 billion just so it can provide the public with faster internet service at a lower cost. It has to recover that investment, which cannot be done by lowering the charges for using its networks. These are hard-nosed businesses we are talking about, not NGOs. End of the Editorial.

This is Larry Henares adding his two cents to this editorial.

The Philippine Daily Inquirer is right, the duopoly of Manny Pangilinan's Smart Communication and the Ayalas' Globe are not NGOs, they are greedy businessmen who had long and heartlessly exploited the Filipino people, exerting influence on the National Telecommunications Commission to allow them to engage in immoral practices that are not allowed elsewhere in the world. At the outset:

(1) they attempted to perpetuate the practice of charging for missed calls on our cell phones;

(2) for a long time, they were able to charge our calls by the minute or a fraction thereof, instead of by the 6-second pulse;

(3) even today, they cheat those who pay in advance by cancelling, after a short time, the unused balance of they actually paid for;

(4) they charge 12 times the cost and 1/10 the speed of what is charged the netizens of Singapore and Korea, so the Philippines has the HIGHEST COST and the SLOWEST SPEED of Internet in all Asia;

(5) Smart has been able to get complete monopoly of the Internet Exchange, and prevent IX peering as practiced in Hong Kong and Singapore;

(6) on another matter, one company has been able to delay by several years the complete digitalization of the TV Broadcast Industry, because it insisted it is entitled to a better location of frequencies (having gotten what it wants, it is now the leading company hurrying up digitalism, urging costumers to buy the necessary "boxes" for receiving the new broadcasts);

(7) ABS-CBN is allowed to have complete monopoly of our Cable Channels for which they charge an arm and a leg for their services;

(8) GMA-7 is allowed to abuse its franchise privileges by broadcasting 30 minutes of advertisements for every hour of broadcast time, almost TWICE the 18 minutes maximum of ads per hour done by other stations.

Information Technology is an activity of highest marginal productivity, creating more wealth with the least input of resources. It requires only Brain Power which has created most of the modern fortunes in the world, and of which we have as much as any country in the planet.

In the first 100 days of the new administration, let us:

(1) immediately DIGITALIZE our broadcasting facilities as we have already decided, reassigning frequencies where 4 high

definition broadcast facilities can exist instead of one low definition facility;

(2) immediately contract the Chinese to supply the broadband digital highway that the Arroyo administration was accused of trying to make money on;

(3) immediately institute Internet Exchange Peering as Hong Kong does, and frustrate internet exchange monopoly of one firm which charges netizens 12 times the cost at 1/10 the Internet speed that Singapore firms provide.
July 11-12, 2016

Part 8. They Don't Know Digong Duterte, by Ramon Tulfo

The notorious bandit group Abu Sayyaf will pay dearly for beheading Canadian hostage Robert Hall to embarrass incoming President Rodrigo "Digong" Duterte. Clearly, they don't know Mano Digong.

Unlike President Noynoy, whom the Abu Sayyaf bandits consider a weakling, Mano Digong is capable of matching—or even surpassing—their violence and cruelty. The only way for the government to deal with those Moro bad boys is to be like them.

The Tausugs, who are Muslims from Sulu, respect non-Muslims or Christians who can match their penchant for violence. If a Tausug beheads your brother, you should retaliate in kind; no ifs and buts about it. Abu Sayyaf bandits are mostly Tausugs.

Retired Lt. Gen. Salvador Mison, who's now a top executive in a big company, knows the Tausug psyche only too well.

When Mison was commander of an Army brigade in Jolo in the 1970s, an inter-island ship carrying more than a hundred passengers was hijacked by members of the Moro National Liberation Front (MNLF). The rebels held the ship passengers hostage and demanded ransom for their release.

Mison tried to talk them into releasing their captives but the rebels threatened to kill everyone if their ransom demand was not met. The next day, then Colonel Mison boarded the ship and told the hostage-takers that he had all their relatives—mothers, fathers, uncles, aunts, wives and children—in custody. "Kill your hostages and I will kill all of your loved ones," Mison warned. The hostages were promptly released.

I hate to recall the atrocities committed during the MNLF rebellion from the 1970s up to the 1980s. But perhaps the Abu Sayyaf, which was nonexistent at that time, could learn a lesson from the distant past.

When the MNLF went rampaging in Mindanao in the early 1970s, nobody could stop them. The Marcos government, caught unprepared, hurriedly trained battalions and battalions of soldiers in Luzon for deployment to Mindanao.

A group of hardy farmers in the Cotabato provinces, mostly Ilongos from Panay Island, held the fort for the government so that Cotabato, with its predominantly Christian population, could not be overrun. The capture by the MNLF of Cotabato would mean that other adjoining Christian provinces and cities in Mindanao would be next to fall.

The Visayan farmers were not as well-armed as the MNLF rebels who had sophisticated arms brought in from the Middle East via Malaysia. But the Christian farmers, who called themselves "ilaga" or rats, surpassed the MNLF rebels in bravery and violence. When the MNLF beheaded and killed Christian captives, the *Ilaga* retaliated in kind and on a bigger scale. For every dead Christian, they killed 10 Moro civilians.

The Ilaga also conducted a bizarre ritual in front of captured MNLF rebels: They disemboweled their dead MNLF captives and ate their cooked innards. Uneducated Moros at that time believed that if any of their body part was missing when they died, they would not be able to enter heaven.

As a result, most MNLF members lost their will to fight the Ilaga.

If I know Mano Digong, the incoming Duterte administration would not be averse to copying what the Ilaga did.

I hope I'm wrong.

Ten battalions or 5,000 soldiers have been deployed in Sulu province to go after the Abu Sayyaf bandits who beheaded two Canadian hostages after their ransom demand was not met.

Even if the government puts 100 battalions in Sulu, the Abu Sayyaf bandits will not be captured.

Why? Because the bandits have the support and sympathy of the local folk who are their relatives or fellow Muslims.

The solution is to put Sulu under martial law and place a total embargo on the island so that goods and people can't enter or leave the province.

Navy ships and numerous "kumpit" —very fast Moro boats that carry barter-trade goods—can surround the island province to intercept people who try to leave.

Boats leaving or entering the province should be sunk after ample warning has been issued for them to stop.

The military can engage in hamletting, a strategy of isolating barrio people from contact with members of an armed group.

Hamletting was used by the British during the anti-insurgency campaign in Malaya in the 1950s and was highly successful.

The Malayan insurgents, deprived of their source of food and moral support, surrendered if they were not yet killed during battles with government troops.

The government can also offer hefty cash reward for people who pinpoint Abu Sayyaf bandits or their relatives in villages under the influence of the bandit group.

The relatives of Abu Sayyaf bandits might be held as pawns for the freedom of their hostages.

The financial reward will come from the military intelligence fund. ***

Of course, the strategic hamlet program should be scrapped after all the Abu Sayyaf bandits are either killed or captured.

From incoming presidential spokesperson, lawyer Salvador Panelo has been moved to chief presidential legal adviser, a designation he will hold after Davao City Mayor Rodrigo "Digong" Duterte takes his oath as president.

Panelo is an unskilled mouthpiece of Mano Digong.

Instead of softening Mano Digong's cuss-laden quarrel with the media, Panelo exacerbated it by adding his own two cents' worth.

Good riddance!

Ernesto Abella, a former clergyman, has replaced Panelo while Martin Andanar, a famous broadcast journalist, as the incoming chief of the Presidential Communications Office.

I don't know much about Abella, except that Mayor

Digong once saved him from his kidnappers, but I know Andanar will be able to reconcile the President-elect with the media because he's one of them.

Digong's quarrel with the Manila media -- he's friendly with reporters in Davao City -- stems from a misunderstanding or miscommunication.

When the Manila media get to know Mano Digong better they'll find him very amiable and a man with a terrific sense of humor.

I should know; I used to dislike the guy.
July 28-29, 2018. UNTV

Part 9. President's Inaugural Speech

My countrymen: No leader, however strong, can succeed at anything of national importance or significance unless he has the support and cooperation of the people he is tasked to lead and sworn to serve.

It is the people from whom democratic governments draw strength and this administration is no exception. That is why we have to listen to the murmurings of the people, feel their pulse, supply their needs and fortify their faith and trust in us whom they elected to public office.

There are many amongst us who advance the assessment that the problems that bedevil our country today which need to be addressed with urgency, are corruption, both in the high and low echelons of government, criminality in the streets, and the rampant sale of illegal drugs in all strata of Philippine society and the breakdown of law and order. True, but not absolutely so. For I see these ills as mere symptoms of a virulent social disease that creeps and cuts into the moral fiber of Philippine society. I sense a problem deeper and more serious than any of those mentioned or all of them put together. But of course, it is not to say that we will ignore them because they have to be stopped by all means that the law allows.

Erosion of faith and trust in government – that is the real problem that confronts us. Resulting therefrom, I see the erosion of the people's trust in our country's leaders; the erosion of faith in our judicial system; the erosion of confidence in the capacity of our public servants to make the people's lives better, safer and healthier.

Indeed, ours is a problem that dampens the human spirit. But all is not lost.

I know that there are those who do not approve of my methods of fighting criminality, the sale and use of illegal drugs and corruption. They say that my methods are unorthodox and verge on the illegal. In response let me say this:

I have seen how corruption bled the government of funds, which were allocated for the use in uplifting the poor from the mire that they are in.

I have seen how illegal drugs destroyed individuals and ruined family relationships.

I have seen how criminality, by means all foul, snatched from the innocent and the unsuspecting, the years and years of accumulated savings. Years of toil and then, suddenly, they are back to where they started.

Look at this from that perspective and tell me that I am wrong.

In this fight, I ask Congress and the Commission on Human Rights and all others who are similarly situated to allow us a level of governance that is consistent to our mandate. The fight will be relentless and it will be sustained.

As a lawyer and a former prosecutor, I know the limits of the power and authority of the president. I know what is legal and what is not.

My adherence to due process and the rule of law is uncompromising.

You mind your work and I will mind mine.

"Compassion. Real change" – these are words which catapulted me to the presidency. These slogans were conceptualized not for the sole purpose of securing the votes of the electorate. Real change. This is the direction of our government.

Far from that. These were battle cries articulated by me in behalf of the people hungry for genuine and meaningful change. But the change, if it is to be permanent and significant, must start with us and in us.

To borrow the language of F. Sionil Jose, we have become our own worst enemies. And we must have the courage and the will to change ourselves.

Love of country, subordination of personal interests to the

common good, concern and care for the helpless and the impoverished – these are among the lost and faded values that we seek to recover and revitalize as we commence our journey towards a better Philippines. The ride will be rough. But come and join me just the same. Together, shoulder to shoulder, let us take the first wobbly steps in this quest.

There are two quotations from revered figures that shall serve as the foundation upon which this administration shall be built.

"The test of government is not whether we add more to the abundance of those who have much; it is whether we provide for those who have little." – Franklin Delano Roosevelt

And from (Abraham) Lincoln I draw this expression: "You cannot strengthen the weak by weakening the strong; You cannot help the poor by discouraging the rich; You cannot help the wage earner by pulling down the wage payer; You cannot further the brotherhood by inciting class hatred among men."

My economic and financial, political policies are contained in those quotations, though couched in general terms. Read between the lines. I need not go into specifics now. They shall be supplied to you in due time.

However, there are certain policies and specifics of which cannot wait for tomorrow to be announced.

Therefore, I direct all department secretaries and the heads of agencies to reduce requirements and the processing time of all applications, from the submission to the release. I order all department secretaries and heads of agencies to remove redundant requirements and compliance with one department or agency, shall be accepted as sufficient for all.

I order all department secretaries and heads of agencies to refrain from changing and bending the rules government contracts, transactions and projects already approved and awaiting implementation. Changing the rules when the game is on-going is wrong.

I abhor secrecy and instead advocate transparency in all government contracts, projects and business transactions from submission of proposals to negotiation to perfection and finally, to consummation.

Do them and we will work together. Do not do them, we will part sooner than later.

On the international front and community of nations, let me reiterate that the Republic of the Philippines will honor treaties and international obligations.

On the domestic front, my administration is committed to implement all signed peace agreements in step with constitutional and legal reforms.

I am elated by the expression of unity among our Moro brothers and leaders, and the response of everyone else to my call for peace. I look forward to the participation of all other stakeholders, particularly our indigenous peoples, to ensure inclusivity in the peace process.

Let me remind in the end of this talk, that I was elected to the presidency to serve the entire country. I was not elected to serve the interests of any one person or any group or any one class. I serve every one and not only one.

That is why I have adapted as an article of faith, the following lines written by someone whose name I could no longer recall. He said: "I have no friends to serve, I have no enemies to harm." I now ask everyone, and I mean everyone, to join me as we embark on this crusade for a better and brighter tomorrow.

Why am I here? I am here because I love my country and I love the people of the Philippines. I am here because I am ready to start my work for the nation. I thank you.
August 1, 2016

Part 10.   A Rousing Start, from an Inquirer Editorial, comment by Henares

The presidency of Rodrigo Roa Duterte is off to a very good start, with a powerfully argued inaugural address that set forth his vision of governance in clear, compelling terms.

Many of us watching the live broadcast or the livestream of the inauguration—only the fifth regularly scheduled inauguration under the 1987 Constitution, and only the sixth when Gloria Arroyo's oath-taking at the Edsa Shrine in 2001 is included—must have braced ourselves for fiery rhetoric, off-script insults, or the occasional expletive, but true to his word, Mr. Duterte underwent a "metamorphosis" in the first hour of his presidency.

He delivered a carefully written, well-calibrated speech— and yet it did not for a moment sound inauthentic. It was the real

Duterte, the veteran prosecutor who was equally at home in English and the language of the law, the successful local executive who proudly points to both his law and order record and his city's thriving example, the long-time politician who has thought often about the country's biggest problems.

Careful, calibrated, and also surprising. The first surprise came early. He listed the issues his presidential campaign was most identified with: "There are many amongst us who advance the assessment that the problems that bedevil our country today which need to be addressed with urgency, are corruption, both in the high and low echelons of government, criminality in the streets, and the rampant sale of illegal drugs in all strata of Philippine society and the breakdown of law and order."

And then he said: "True, but not absolutely so."

He said he detected a "virulent social disease" that was "deeper and more serious"—the people's "erosion of faith and trust in government," he said, was "the real problem that confronts us."

We can disagree with this reading (and we do; the surveys, the record-high voter turnout, and the victory of a career politician support the opposite view) and yet we can still appreciate the new President's point. We all expect more from our government, and the Duterte presidency is premised on making those expectations come true.

To be completely fair, all administrations have started out with similar premises and promises; we must test the rhetoric against the reality. But it is instructive that a deeper diagnosis of social ills informs the Duterte campaign's emphasis on fighting crime and corruption.

In measured terms, President Duterte referenced his iron-fist reputation. "I know that there are those who do not approve of my methods ... They say that my methods are unorthodox and verge on the illegal." (Some criticism asserts that he has in fact gone over the verge.) He then offered an impassioned rationale for his methods—"I have seen how illegal drugs destroyed individuals and ruined family relationships"—before addressing the human rights issue that haunts his record.

"In this fight, I ask Congress and the Commission on Human Rights and all others who are similarly situated to allow us a level of governance that is consistent to our mandate .... As a lawyer and a former prosecutor, I know the limits of the power and authority of the president. I know what is legal and what is not. My adherence to due process and the rule of law is uncompromising."

We appreciate the President's reiteration of his commitment to due process and the rule of law, and his appeal to Congress and the CHR to "mind their work." But we also note that he did not include the courts in his request for a mandate-consistent level of governance. This is a good sign, that his reputation as a courteous respecter of the judiciary's prerogatives is not without basis. Mr. Duterte ended his address, surprisingly, with quotes from two American presidents. The one from Franklin Roosevelt is positively Magsaysay-esque: The true test of government is "whether we provide for those who have little." This helps explain why the new administration will likely be characterized by an emphasis on social justice. The passage from Abraham Lincoln gives the assurance that social justice will not come at the expense of any other sector of society: "You cannot strengthen the weak by weakening the strong."

Between the philosophies of these two political giants—the greatest American president of the 20th century and the greatest of the 19th—President Duterte must manage a difficult balancing act. But it is fair to say that, by the end of his stirring inaugural address, there were more people rooting for him. End of Editorial.

This is Larry Henares contributing his two cents worth to this editorial for the remnants of the PNoy Administration – Chairman of the Commission of Human Rights Chito Gascon and Vice President Leni Robredo, using the words of Teddyboy Locsin, one of the best writers of our time, known for his wit and wisdom and flair for irony.

To Chito Gascon: They say that the reason you are in that office is that you are the husband of Belmonte's secretary, that you don't have even a law degree, and have been nitpicking on Duterte just to get newspaper space. "What is wrong with shoot-to-kill? If someone poses a mortal threat, like armed robbers who threaten lives, or drug pushers who destroy lives, it is not unnatural to issue shoot-to-kill orders. What if it gets out of hand? This is the doctrine of the "slippery slope" in constitutional law. It is like this. If your authority to stop something extends to a radius of say 10 feet, you may go as far as 8 feet only, because 9 is too close to 10, and 10 can spill over from legitimate law enforcement to abuse of power. So with shoot-to-kill orders, some may slide down from killing criminals to killing political enemies or killing critical journalists. It should not happen. But you can always tell one from the other. You cannot always slip from one to the other without someone noticing the legal difference on the basis of human experience and practical wisdom, and attacking you for it. So, let Duterte threaten to issue any order he likes. And wait and see. If it results in deterring crime, well and good. But if it results in something criminal, he will be impeached. Trust me on this. This will happen even if he has Congress in his pocket.

To Leni Robredo: You advocate Unity with the Duterte administration, suggesting a political honeymoon. "They say the Unity is essential to Progress. No, Diversity is the spark of Creativity and Competition is the lifeblood of the Economy. Unity is for slaves, to pull in the same direction under the lash. In a free country and a free economy, unity leads to collective catastrophe and cartels. The one in the lead will always take us in the wrong direction, that is to say, into his pocket. The idea of leadership is abhorrent to free men. Leadership is for tribes, for guys who do not wear trousers. Wolves attack in packs, lions in prides, but only for convenience. Wolves and lions attack each other all the time, not for leadership, but for the biggest slice of the pie. Believe me, there is no such thing as a honeymoon in a democracy. In a honeymoon, someone always gets screwed." So do what you were elected for. Be in the opposition.
August 3-4, 2016, UNTV

Part 11. Simplicity is for simpletons, by Teodoro Locsin Jr.

You are what you read, says a study in the International Journal of Business Administration. Read deep, think deep; read complicated things, think complicated thoughts. The world is complicated. Read simple stuff; limit your understanding to simple things. The world is not at all simple.

The best proof of the depth and complexity of your thinking is not the simplicity but the clarity with which you express depth and complexity. Simplicity is not clarity. What we really want is clarity.

Deep reading cuts into your soul and shapes you like real life experiences. Few of us have deep experiences but we can all read about them and thereby experience them; in my view better—with the wisdom of those who actually lived them and the luxury of reflection.

We may never meet wise people; most of them are dead; but we can converse with them by reading their deep and difficult writings. That is the kind of reading that changes you.

But if you read only simple stuff, it will bring immediate pleasure; but only a passing and shallow understanding of our complex world.

I am saying this because we now have a president who will influence what we read and therefore how we think. His partiality for brevity and clarity might be mistaken for superficiality and simplemindedness. This president is the farthest from that. He has lived through the most tumultuous times of our country. He has heard the tattered banners of opposing camps beating in the hurricane winds of our politics and conflicts.

He says little but speaks volumes. Taken in isolation, his surprisingly complicated words shout of the sufferings of our people, and speak faintly of the hopes they are giving up. He alludes to imperialism, capitalism, anarchy and order, judicial incapacity and extrajudicial solutions, and democracy that is a parody of itself. These words contain a history that baffles common understanding and frustrates the discovery, and the adoption, of effective solutions.

We have a thinking president. Let us make the effort to think as hard as he does.

Make no mistake. Whether he has read the situation rightly or wrongly, he will proceed to act on the conclusions he has arrived at with much hard thought and deep reflection.

So he will not stop, unless we can give him a compelling reason to stop, and also a better way to achieve the good ends he seeks.

He is old. I sense he is tired. But he is resolved that, while there is breath in him, not just to talk change like past presidents, but make change. And die in the trying.

If we do not take advantage of this man's leadership, we shall miss our last chance of real change.

Dr. Hilarion M. Henares Jr.   **143**

August, 2016

Part 12. To the Point, by Teodoro Locsin Jr.

We now know that our President speaks plainly and to the point, so much so that he is really pissed that we still don't get him. Before he said goodbye to Davao on his way to his inauguration as Mayor of the Republic, Duterte repeated what he has been saying all along, to wit, "I will kill you if you hurt my people, if you hurt my country. I am talking to you drug pushers, drug users, to violent criminals in general, and to the police who protect them all." Like the Syrian police who protected the murderer of a retired US serviceman during a home invasion. The Syrian police told the surviving victims to investigate the crime themselves, to find the evidence, and to file the case against the killer they are protecting and whom they let go.

That said, whoever wants to write for or write to President Duterte better learn the rules of short and clear messaging, because the man will only listen to someone who talks like him.

The original adman David Ogilvy, the greatest PR man, has good advice on how to do that, with a little help from me. The better you write, the higher you go in the President's esteem, because people who think well, write well. Wooly minded people write wooly memos, wooly letters and wooly speeches. Good writing is not a natural gift, you have to learn it. Here are ten hints:

1.   Read books on good writing, there a few classics. Read your favorite three times.

2.   Write the way you talk or should talk, which is to say, naturally, and I may add, to the point. Do not beat around the bush. Beating around the bush means, as the saying goes, masturbation or self-abuse.

3. Use short words like "kill"; short sentences like "I will kill you"; short paragraphs like "I will kill you. Continue what you are doing, and see if I am serious."

4. Do not use jargon words like reconstructionize, securitize, you are my bosses, paradigm shift. These are hallmarks of pretentious assholes who never understood the context where such words first appeared.

5. Never write more than 2 pages on any subject, even an inaugural speech. I wrote Cory's inaugural on the spot, on one side of a napkin at Club Filipino.

6. Check your quotation. I would add, paraphrase if you are a writing genius, and probably improve the original.

7. Never send a letter or a memo on the day you write it. Read it aloud the morning after and edit it, or throw it away.

8. If it is that important, get a colleague to improve it.

9. Before sending your letter or memo, be sure it is crystal clear what you want the recipient to do.

10. If you want action, don't write, go and tell the guy what you want, face to face, especially if it is a good thing but extra-judicial.

Thank David and myself. That is all.

August 2016

PART 13. Proposal for Urban Decongestion
Urban Renewal

Wow! You should see the plan submitted by NEDA in collaboration with Japan International Cooperation Agency (JICA), entitled "Mega Manila Infrastructure Roadmap." To say the least the plan is awesome, so well thought out, so well planned. Google it, view it with wonder and admiration. The plan involves Metro Manila which produces 36% of the nation's GDP, and together with Region 3 and 4A, as the Greater Capital Region, or Mega Manila, produces 62 percent of the national GDP.

The plan seeks to solve the area's three major intertwined and interacting problems: Transport (traffic congestion and poor traffic safety); Environment (risk of floods, earthquakes, landslides, and decreased open space, and air pollution); Land Use (urban sprawl, lack of affordable housing, poor living environment).

Let us focus for a moment on the need of Affordable Housing. We have a backlog of 500,000 households, and in addition we need to resettle 556,000 households. This needs to be solved IMMEDIATELY because Metro Manila's population which is 12 million at present is projected to increase to 14 million in 2030, at the same time Mega Manila increases from 23 million to 30 million population.

How to accommodate people in need of affordable housing, free of hazard risks and traffic congestion? We take issue on how the NEDA plans to handle the Urban Poor's re-settlement, livelihood and future. The Urban Poor face imminent relocation when the Government's Public Private Partnership [PPP] plans for Mega Manila begin. We know too well the methods and ways our Government have handled re-locations in the past, as in the aftermath of the Yolanda typhoon disaster. Government re-locations end at demolition and eviction. "*Pantawid*" ways of measly dole-outs don't work.

What needs to be done, and what we propose to do is to relocate the families on the SAME DAY that their shanties are demolished. We will provide temporary housing on in-City sites, and in 7 years we will transfer them to New Towns in the outlying suburbs from where they will have available transportation to get back to their jobs in Metro Manila. During all that time, we will provide JOBS for most of them. And we shall do this without a single cent outlay from the government, and taking all the necessary risks involved. As African-American economist Thomas Sowell once wrote: "It is hard to imagine a more stupid or more dangerous way of making decisions than by putting those decisions in the hands of people who pay no price for being wrong."

VanGO Housing.
Central to this plan is the manufacture of VanGO housing units from ubiquitous 40-ft. and 20-ft. container vans used for international shipping. These vans are made of steel impervious to sea-water; they are strong and weather-proof. These vans can be modified into modular housing units, 40 feet by 8 feet, having 320 square feet of living space, consisting of two rooms plus bath and living/dining area, completely piped for water, electricity, sewerage, TV and internet connection. These Van-Go modular units are assembled to form 5-story, walk-up, medium-rise buildings, completely earthquake/fire/storm proof, with more than 50 years service life. They can be disassembled and transported by truck or train for re-location anywhere.

Imagine, one of these VanGO units occupy the space taken up by 5 shanties that it replaces. It can be manufactured in great quantities and assembled in record time so that we can actually guarantee that the urban poor will be housed on the very same day their shanties are demolished. With the saving of land space, we can give them homes inside the city limits, so that their life style and livelihoods may not be unduly impaired.

In-City Temporary relocation sites.

If we are to eliminate and avoid the threat, risk and harm consequential to eviction, we have to provide the urban poor temporary 7-year relocation sites within Greater Manila Area. These In-City relocation sites are used only for a period of 5 to 7 years as a transition stage to their permanent relocation to NewTowns. In-City relocation does not prejudice their present source of income and livelihood or the social capital that they have nurtured and trusted for years.

More than 2,000 hectares of buildable areas can be created within Greater Manila. with a linear length exceeding 50 kilometers, as TEMPORARY instant relocation sites for 800,000 families. All these from the covered rivers and creeks of the 11 Public/Private/Partnership projects, which we will use to erect the temporary medium-rise buildings of VanGO units. These are the San Juan, Malabon, and Upper Marikina Rivers; the Mangahan spillway, Tripa de Gallina; and other connected esteros/creeks in the Greater Manila Area.

Additionally, we may use the present areas occupied by squatters, saving 4/5 of the space with the use of VanGO modular Units, provided of course, this does not interfere with government projects like the 11 PPP anti-flood mitigation projects.

Also we may build on unused government-owned city land in the University of the Philippines, Quezon City, National Development Corporation, etcetera. Also on foreclosed properties of government owned financial institutions. Or above/below the Rights of Way of Metropolitan Waterworks and Sewerage System, National Power Corp., Philippine National Railways, Department of Public Works and Highways, and above sealed-off esteros, creeks and rivers. Not to worry, we will lease existing properties under a renewable 25-year lease, and have a perpetual usufruct on land we created by building over creeks, esteros and rivers. We will undertake to fund and bear all the incremental infrastructure cost for In-City relocation sites.

Permanent NewTowns. Within 5 to 7 years, after the permanent suburban NewTowns are completed, we will dismantle, transport by truck or rail, and relocate the VanGO units to new locations. This plan offers a unique opportunity to craft innovative solutions to handle both the NEDA Priority projects, beyond mere relocation of the Urban Poor.

The number of houses for each NewTown will be such as to be viable for the needed services such as water, sewerage, telephone, power, internet and TV connections, markets, health centers, police protection, schools, parks, sports facilities, garbage disposal. The NewTown site must be chosen with special attention to its interconnection to the City. Imperative is the support and cooperation of the Local Government Units. Should the ideal property be privately owned, we will seek the government's use of its Right of Eminent Domain to acquire said property, based on its present real estate tax valuation. We will undertake all expenses to build the interconnecting highway and establish a point-to-point transport system to and from NewTown to the nearest MRT/LRT/ railway. Strict discipline is necessary in NewTowns, like a military school. We will employ the same organization and discipline practices, as has been proven by well-run privately owned enterprises in industry and commerce. The benefits the people will receive are predicated on their compliance to our rules and regulations.

We will begin building NewTowns in the suburbs and complete them within 5 to 7 years to accommodate the relocation of the Urban Poor. Each NewTown community will be run like a Cooperative, to take full advantage of government tax incentives. ###

Livelihood Projects. Our goal is for each urban poor beneficiary to be financially independent as soon as possible. All jobs created in the manufacture and installation of VanGO housing units and the preparation, operation and maintenance of the NewTown will preferentially be given to the relocated urban poor and their families. Not only do they get on-the-job-training but with the cooperation of TESDA, they will also be given training to promote productivity and discipline in the work they are assigned to do, and given certificates of competency useful in applying for other jobs.

They and their family members will also be given a chance to learn such skills needed by barbers, shoe makers and repairers, laundrymen, gardeners, drivers, caregivers, midwives, and other service providers needed by the NewTown community. Each family must have the means and familiarity on the use of state of the art communication devices (cell phone, computer and internet connection) as an aid to whatever they need to know.   Preferential rights to store locations and jobs in the markets and commercial centers are also theirs for the taking.

But this enterprise is not for charity. Each beneficiary will be charged rent for the house and lot he occupies. A contract to sell will be entered with the head of the family and the property will be sold to them as soon as their household income can qualify them for borrowing. Quality education will be made available. And scholarships and job opportunities will be granted to the deserving. But the beneficiaries will be required to render tasks/works assigned to them and observe rules and regulations. A portion of their income will be used to gradually pay back their obligation. Everyone will be encouraged to be independent, responsible, and be the best he can be.

Funding the "HEAL the Philippines Foundation."

A Foundation will be organized by three persons: Arturo Carlos, the originator of this project; Sixto Roxas III and Hilarion M. Henares Jr., both former Chairmen of the National Economic Council.   Eventually it will be controlled and managed by a consortium of businessmen, led by the Henry Sy, Jaime Zobel, Manuel Pangilinan, Andrew Tan, etc., if they so desire. What we really need is not their cash, but their business judgment and competence in management, and willingness to be jointly and severally liable, to guarantee payment of all obligations.

The principal source of funding will come from the SECURITIZATION of INWARD REMITTANCES in the same way Brazil originated and operated the process. The Foundation will buy the Philippine Postal Savings Bank, which will consolidate all inward foreign exchange remittances and securitize 10% of them, raising approximately $26 Billion or ONE Trillion Pesos, which will be given to the Foundation in exchange of Bonds to finance its program of urban renewal, urban re-engineering and anti-flooding,   by   way   of   Public/Private/Partnership. Build/Operate/Transfer, and Build/Operate/Own.

The Foundation will own the air-rights acquired from the Government such as the renewable usufructs used In-City sites for VanGO housing; the 75% of the common areas of

NewTowns, usufructs on other Rights Of Way; the receivables from the Urban Poor which will be repaid from their future income; and the investment returns from the Public/Private/Partnership projects entered into by the Foundation. These are essential assets needed to back-up the outstanding Bonds the Foundation will issue. The Foundation needs the support of the Government, especially from the Bangko Sentral, Public Works, Interior and Local Governments, National Housing, National Power, Social Security, PAGIBIG, Social Welfare, Agrarian Reform, etcetera.

This is a Private Undertaking

Since this is brought about by PRIVATE INITIATIVE, our Government will not be burdened to raise funding/borrowings or to implement new tax measures. Why this must be a PRIVATE UNDERTAKING: time-proven capitalist-driven organizations alone can and do deliver performance. The managerial discipline and practices of private enterprises, where investors and managers are jointly and severally liable for ALL RISK, are able to create the innovations and economic advances we have today. The competitive nature of Capitalism demands performance to survive and prevail; it is the reward and punishment, incentives and compensation, and inevitable bankruptcy for failure – which no government entity can really experience. Graft and corruption prevails in government-managed operations. Even under PNoy's *Daan Matuwid*, we still experience corruption at the MRT. Again we quote Thomas Sowell, **"It is hard to imagine a more stupid or more dangerous way of making decisions than by putting those decisions in the hands of people who pay no price for being wrong."**

Our operation will involve using and adapting the best managerial tools and practices, just as we too will adapt and use the most effective ways to transform our Urban Poor to be responsible and mature Filipinos.

We shall build NewTowns with resilience to cope with disasters, climate change, violence, and economic and political shocks, while maintaining the operational capacity to respond to any challenge when needed; we shall build communities that will uphold humanitarian principles, and citizens who will imbibe moral and ethical values that will promote an economic miracle, a social revolution, and a democratic renaissance – moral behavior to be followed in their hearts and minds, not only on weekends, but every day, every hour and every minute of their lives – to instill not only love of God, but also a sense of right and wrong, proper interpersonal relations, national self-discipline, a desirable work ethic, and above all, love of country.

How to raise money without government bonds or taxes.

There are two urban legends that persist in our imagination, the man who put his foot in his mouth, and the man who shot himself in the foot. A cousin of mine is the only man we know who actually shot his own foot with a Ruger 357, a true urban legend, and in our estimation, a unique person with an artificial foot and the brain of a genius. His name is Arturo Carlos, and this project of urban renewal and re-engineering is his idea. Central to this project is his proposal to raise a trillion pesos, without Bangko Sentral liability though sale of government bonds, or the Congress raising taxes.

The Overseas Filipino Workers (OFW) are considered national heroes because together they are mainly responsible for the steady inward flow of dollars that fuel our economy, some $26 billion a year income cash flow. Steady cash flow can be securitized, as Brazil once did, sold as bonds in the international market, and converted to cash for developmental purposes. How may this be done?

First we funnel all inward remittances of $26 billion through one entity, and securitize 10% of them, or $2.6 billion. In the stock market, the market value of any stock is based on its profitability. An asset is valued as a multiple of its annual profit. In the same way, a profit cash flow of $2.6b has a market value of 10 times or $26b. This asset is converted into private bonds, duly and highly rated by an agency like Fitch, sold in the international market, and converted into cash for our project, $26b or approximately one trillion pesos. Not bad, eh?

I was invited to a gathering for lunch of old and ailing people, and among them was an old friend, Conrado "Ben" Sanchez Jr., an economist who was once the head of the Export Department of the Central Bank. I spoke to him of our proposal for Urban Renewal, with the hope of soliciting a peer review of its validity and viability. He listened and said, "It is a great plan and it should work, but it won't. Your partner Ting Roxas should know. He had many excellent proposals, involving land use and cattle-raising that never got off the planning stage. It won't work because (1) Filipino national leaders don't listen, (2) Filipino bureaucrats are corrupt, and (3) Filipino businessmen are too greedy."

My friend revealed that he has clouded vision due to cataracts, and is battling advanced diabetes, and failing kidneys which necessitate undergoing dialysis in the coming week. At his advanced age, his doctors advise him not to undergo the procedure, but he insists anyway. I realized then that my friend is about to die, that his words were freighted with urgency and meaning when he said, "Please listen to me, Larry. I have done my best to serve my country. I can claim credit for having initiated the export of electronics, textiles, and Filipino overseas workers (our top dollar earners). But to accomplish these, I had to go abroad and talk to foreign officials and foreign businessmen, not to my boss who was corrupt, not to local businessmen who are greedy, and insist on protection and unjust advantage."

He is right of course. Art Carlos, Ting Roxas and I had this proposal for Urban Renewal long time ago, but officials for mass housing rejected it outright, having their rackets to protect. We approached those who deplore official corruption and offer "*daan matuwid*" in governance. But despite having been Presidential Consultant on National Affairs to two presidents, and having served all presidents since Magsaysay, I failed to state my case. Secretary Mar Roxas and Vice President Jojo Binay, who are friends of mine, were much much too busy, to afford even the smallest suggestion of the faintest shadow or suspicion of anything remotely approaching the time or the inclination to listen to our proposal. The few times I and my son Atom had the attention of President NoyNoy Aquino, he did most of the talking, and everyone else listened. I have to remind myself that I am 92 years old, that Ting Roxas and Art Carlos are in their 80s. There is absolutely no time for us to see this grand project through in our lifetimes.

Grand Strategy of how to get it done.

We campaigned and voted for Duterte's promise of "Pagbabago." Maybe, just maybe, President Rodrigo R. Duterte, having appointed Vice President Leni Robredo as Housing Czar, may endorse this proposal for Urban Renewal to her, not only for mass housing but also as a chance to decongest Metro Manila and utilize his emergency powers to solve the traffic problem to set the stage for its fruition… Mass Housing, Urban Renewal, and Traffic Decongestion all achieved in one fell swoop.

We will speak to Henry Sy, Jaime Zobel, Manuel Pangilinan, Ramon Ang and other tycoons, and give them an offer they cannot refuse: "We ask for no cash, only for your credit standing. We will raise for your consortium One Trillion Pesos. You assemble the best and the brightest management team to give our people affordable housing and NewTowns, ease the traffic congestion, clean the environment for Mega Manila, and jointly and severally take the responsibility for success or failure."
August 8-12, 2016, UNTV

PART 14. ENDO and the right to hire and fire

Memorandum to President Rodrigo R. Duterte; Labor Secretary Sylvestre Bello III, Finance Secretary Carlos Dominguez, Trade and Industry Secretary Ramon Lopez.
Dated Thursday, August 8, 2016, **Re:** <u>ENDO and the right to hire and fire</u>

The real engine of growth and development is not government but business and private initiative. Business combines money, machines and materials to achieve prosperity for the entire nation, like no other. Business provides (1) goods for the consumers, (2) jobs for the unemployed, (3) profits for the investors, and (4) tax income for the government. Corruption in its most virulent form is a government that impedes the honest and efficient practice of business. And such corruption infests all levels of government. We are gratified that you have set your policy against all corruption, including complicated and useless regulations, and now the patent abuse of contractualization to avoid paying workers what they are entitled to by law. We think that this was adopted by business to defend itself from onerous provisions of the labor law.

What prevents foreign investors from investing in our country is evident. Unlike in the USA and other countries, where the basic right of employers to hire and fire employees without government intervention is respected, in the Philippines employers are answerable to a quasi-judicial National Labor Relations Commission (NLRC) which adjudicates employment disputes -- something only socialist governments have.

This gave rise to alleged rackets by employees and labor lawyers in collusion with government officials, to extort money from business. One employer complains that after catching employees using drugs in the work-place, he was mandated to provide expensive rehabilitation for them instead of firing them on the spot. Another employer, out of charity for an old woman, by giving her the privilege of cleaning the public toilet and charging fees from the users, for 25 years, after having been being paid extra on 3 occasions for work as a messenger, was ordered by the court to give back-pay to the woman in the hundreds of thousands of pesos, for alleged unpaid wages. That is outright extortion! Inefficient, lazy and undesirable employees mock their employers with an attitude of "Catch me if you can."

We suggest that employers and employees work together in a Christian spirit, to adopt a system beneficial to both employer and employee. We propose that if a person is fired, he be given a monetary aid in accordance to law. In this law, it must be provided that an erring employee, or one whose output is sub-standard, should not receive this monetary aid when dismissed. Furthermore, the employee must be made to realize that he totally depends on the employer. Therefore he must work honestly and diligently when hired.

This amount will be graduated or calibrated based solely on tenure, commensurate to how long he has worked for the company. This is to tide him over until he finds another job. In the USA, the right to hire and fire is conditioned by lawful provisions on separation pay. We humbly submit that together with ending the ENDO, the administration also reasserts the right of employers to hire and fire which is sacrosanct in every progressive nation on earth, to wit:

➢ Amend the Labor Code, *Article 211,* Declaration of Policies, with the addition of "*A.h.* to recognize the basic right of the employer to hire and fire employees, subject only to the provisions of the Collective Bargaining Agreement, if any, and to provisions of the Labor Code regarding termination pay and penalties for unfair labor practice.

➢ Amend *Article 279*, Security of Tenure, to read "An employee who is unjustly dismissed is entitled, not to reinstatement, but to termination pay and penalties imposed by the Labor Department for unfair labor practice."
August 8, 2016

PART 15. The Secret Agenda Of Rodrigo Duterte, draft by Henares

On Crime, Peace and Order, And Corruption.

First, I shall have a law passed to restore the Death Penalty for drug pushers. drug-lords, rapists, murderers, any policemen or soldier who kill or kidnap anyone they are supposed to protect, and prison officials who release prisoners to do murder-for-hire. Let us not delude ourselves that our prisons rehabilitate, more often they serve as schools for the furtherance of crime. I do not want the nation to spend resources to feed un-rehabilitable criminals; let us bring back the death penalty to reduce prison population, and bury these incorrigibles in farmland to fertilize the soil, and for once and final time, be of some use to the people they have abused. *REASON: Objections of the Catholic Church and Bleeding Hearts.*

Second, I shall change the mindset of the Armed Forces and the National Police that anyone against the rich oligarchs or against Americans are to be disposed off with extreme prejudice, and I shall ask the Supreme Court to issue a general Writ of Amparo against armed officers kidnapping and/or killing any student, professor, or labor organizer, or any peaceful dissenter.

REASON: Objections from the Fascists among the rich people, and McCarthyists from the Military.

On Traffic Congestion.

First, we shall put high taxes on private cars in Metro Manila, refuse licenses to cars being parked on the streets and have no private place to be garaged in. We will not prioritize the manufacture of cars, knowing that while car sales increase by 25% every years, road space increase only 1.5% a year. *REASON: Objections of the foreign car manufacturers.*

Education and Moral Regeneration.

First, I will convince the Supreme Court to issue a Writ of Amparo against religious organizations that coerce their members to neglect their basic constitutional right to vote freely, and to organize to bargain collectively. I believe that this will level the playing field for all organizations seeking unfair and advantageous political influence. *REASON: Objections of Iglesia ni Cristo and politicians who cater to it, the result of which is the pervasive influence of INC at all levels of the government, specially the Presidency, Congress, Judiciary and police agencies. It is political corruption at its worst, and someday this organization will totally own our government.*

Foreign Policy.

I believe that the so-called Special Relations between the Philippines and the United States began when the first American Rascal met the First Filipino Fool. We are grateful for the Liberation and grant of Independence in 1945. We are grateful to a brilliant American lawyer, Elihu Root, who drafted the directive issued by President McKinley to the Taft Commission, granting the entire Bill of Rights *gratis et amore* including the magnificent First Amendment (freedom of speech, assembly and worship), the great Fourth (against unreasonable search and seizures), also the wonderful Thirteenth (against involuntary servitude) – giving us Filipinos in one fell swoop in 1901, what the Anglo Saxons fought, bled and died for 450 years since the Magna Carta (1215) in Runnymede to the Habeas Corpus Act in 1640, to the Emancipation Proclamation (1863) after Gettysburg.

But we are disappointed in the Special Relations after we became free and independent. Special relations have never been reciprocal. The parity rights granted in our constitution to all Americans, were never enjoyed by Filipinos anywhere in the USA except in the state of New York. The $3 billion granted to us in 1945 consisted mostly of junk war surplus worth 5 cents to the dollar, war reparations granted mostly to Americans in the Philippines, and Backpay paid in pesos rather than in dollars. We resent CIA interference, the McCarthyist witchhunts, the Low Intensity Conflicts, and the American insistence that we stop industrializing, to serve as a vegetable garden for the industrial economies of Japan, South Korea and Taiwan.

First, I will declare that we Filipinos are no longer the Little Brown Brothers to the White Americans, that we will no longer be slavish to the interests of America at the expense of our own, and will develop free and unaligned relations with all nations;

REASON: Objections of the American carpetbaggers and Filipino scalawags with a colonial mentality.

PART 16.   Proposal for Federal Presidential Unicameral system

Drafted for Dante Liban, Chairman, People's National Movement for Federalism (Penamfed)

A draft of proposed constitutional amendments for a Federal Presidential Unicameral system for the Philippines was submitted to President Duterte for the consideration of the proposed 25-member Constitutional Commission and the Constituent Assembly, by Dante Liban, Chairman of the People's National Movement for Federalism, which has chapters in every part of the country.

Dante Liban says his proposal is in direct opposition to the proposed Federal Parliamentary system advocated by others. "A parliamentary system vests the executive and the legislative powers in a Prime Minister and his cabinet of legislators. But consider our political culture and experience. Our elected legislators not usually the best and brightest; among the most influential members of Congress are political opportunists (balimbings) and the leaders they select are not as good as the presidents we elect. Compare the caliber of any Speaker with that of Presidents Manuel Quezon, Ramon Magsaysay, Diosdado Macapagal, Cory Aquino, Fidel Ramos, and Rodrigo Duterte. There is no contest. The best and the brightest in their fields are usually the appointed Cabinet members, not members of Congress.

"The Prime Minister may be changed any time, but he can also, by means fair or foul, serve indefinitely, forever, with all the resources under his command. I would really prefer that we the people directly elect our leaders than indirectly entrust the function to elected legislators. We are ultimately the most sovereign, and we must never entrust both the legislative and executive power to one man, especially one that can perpetuate himself in power as a leader. In the Philippines, a Prime Minister under a Parliamentary system, finds it easier to buy the support of 250 legislators (not even that, only 126 will suffice) than to court the votes of 20 million Filipinos under a Presidential system. Absolute Power corrupts absolutely," says Dante Liban.

"We believe that that that President Duterte himself was given the ultimate mandate to amend the Constitution to a Federal System, not anyone else. So we insist that the President himself approve his own draft, and use his tremendous influence to get the Constituent Assembly to approve it without change. He knows that a good constitution should include provisions that may not be acceptable to the legislators: (1) an anti-dynasty provision that will specifically forbid the election of a relative within 4 degrees of consanguinity from any elected official by counting the degrees of relationship to and from a common ancestor, as commonly defined; with the added assurance that such relatives forbidden from seeking election may serve the government as appointed officials; (2) one that consolidates the National Capital Region into one State and governed by an elected Governor under the National Government, and like Washington DC: (3) one that forbids any organization, religious or otherwise, from forcing its members to abandon their rights under this bill of rights, especially the right to join a labor union for the purpose of bargaining collectively, and the right to vote for any candidate of their choice – to prevent the corruption of our political, police and judicial systems." Liban continued.

Other provisions included in the draft submitted:

(1) one incorporating into the national territory the Economic Zones mandated by the UN Law of the Sea, Sabah which was stolen from us by the British, and which we should claim in the proper UN Court;

(2) Presidential and Unicameral on both the National and State levels; The National Government will retain all its functions (Armed Forces, Police, Internal Revenue, Customs, Judiciary, etcetera) except the power to invite and regulate foreign and local investment, without the restrictions of the present constitution, (minimum wage, business permits, real estate tax, sales tax, local infrastructures, etcetera) to encourage competition between states;

(3) Except for the President and Vice President who are required to be natural-born with 10 years residence, all other officials are not burdened with residential requirements, or natural-born status, the only requirement being age and status as Filipino citizens. Any Filipino citizen may be chosen to serve any Federal State, even if he is not a resident there. In that way,

for example, an Ilocano ex-President may be recruited for his prestige and experience to serve a Visayan State or any other Federal State;

(4) one provision designating as Federal States the 18 existing Regions plus one comprising Sulu, Basilan and Tawi Tawi, 19 all in all, however the 13 states suggested by Nene Pimentel may be considered.

(5) The National Assembly shall be composed of thirty eight Assemblymen, two of which shall be elected at large by the qualified voters of each of the 19 Federal States; the Federal State Assembly shall be elected by legislative districts within each State, augmented by five more State Assemblymen elected at large within each Federal State.

(6) Eighty percent of National Revenue, after deducting the budget for the National Government and payments for foreign debts, shall be parcelled to the Federal State Governments totally and automatically, on the basis of 50% according to population (to be reapportioned every after the National Census), 15% according to land area and topography, and 15% in equal shares.

(7) We shall abrogate or refuse to extend all unfair and one sided treaties imposed upon us by strong nations. We shall insist on sincere apologies from every nation that has ever violated our human rights and forced to pursue policies against our national interests.

(8) We shall no longer tolerate any nation refusing to confirm or deny bringing nuclear weapons into our territories.

(9) The constitution shall equally protect the basic human rights of women and minorities of every race, color and creed, and persons of different sexual orientations, from the tyranny of the majority.

(10) The state shall promote comprehensive rural development and agrarian reform, and self-sufficient agriculture; and specially industrialization and information technology as the primary mode of economic development.

(11) The state adopts and implements a policy of full public disclosure of all its transactions involving public interest, such disclosure not limited by any privacy laws as far as government officials, appointed and/or elected, are concerned,

subject to no limitations except in matters involving, national security, public safety and/or public health.

(12) No torture, force, violence, threat, intimidation, or any other means which vitiate the free will shall be used against anyone. Secret detention places, solitary, incommunicado, or other similar forms of detention are prohibited, specially by the police and armed forces, who shall be subject up to a maximum penalty of reclusion perpetua and death penalty for this most grievous crime of infidelity to public duty.

(13) The petition for a writ of amparo shall be made available to any person whose right to life, liberty and security is violated or threatened with violation by an unlawful act or omission of a public official or employee, or of a private individual or entity, or of a religious organization.

(14) Among those considered as natural born citizens: those whose fathers or mothers are citizens of the Philippines; those foundlings within the Philippines, who shall be assumed of Filipino parentage, unless proven otherwise; those who are adopted by Filipino parents before the age of 18 years.

(15) Churches shall be exempt from taxation, unless such institutions are engaged in business for profit in competition with the general public.

(16) Sharia Laws shall apply only to those who submit themselves to its jurisdiction, otherwise the National Law shall prevail.

(17) to foster long term economic policy not subject to changes by any president, the constitutional body the National Economic Council in the 1935 Constitution shall be restored, one third of which shall consist of the Premier and two members of the National Assembly; one third consisting of the Secretary of Finance, of Trade and Industry and the Chairman of the Development Bank of the Philippines; and one third consisting of representatives of the private sector (labor, industry and agriculture to be appointed by the President for 7-year terms); headed by a Chairman appointed by the President co-terminus with the Presidential term.

(18) In the exploitation of natural resources, the state limits participation to Filipinos or to corporations or associations at least 40% of whose capital is owned by Filipinos.

(19) the state shall regulate or prohibit monopolies when the public interest so requires. No combinations in restraint of trade or unfair competition shall be allowed. The National Assembly shall enact an Anti-Trust Act similar to the Sherman and Clayton Anti-Trust Laws of the United States.

(20) the state shall regulate the relations between workers and employers, recognizing the right of labor to its just share in the fruits of production and the right of enterprises to reasonable returns on investments, and to expansion and growth; and recognize the basic right of employers to hire and fire, subject only to conditions dictated by the Collective Bargaining Agreement and laws governing Separation Pay and Unfair Labor Practices.

(21) the state shall respect the right of small landowners and corporations formed to engage in modern farming.

(22) the state shall establish legal sanctions against elitist schools discriminating against the admission of students who are children of single parents, divorced or separated parents or of any student on the basis of creed, color or race, and oblige elitist schools to give compulsory scholarships to poor and deserving students.

(23) All educational institutions shall include the study of the Constitution as part of the curricula, shall at all times respect and follow the tenets of basic academic freedoms, specifically forbidding the practice of book burning and author banning at the university level, most specially classic books embodied in such series as the Great Books of Chicago University, and the Harvard Classics. Aliens teaching or supervising Philippine educational institutions should be required to learn to speak Wikang Pilipino or some native dialect to better communicate and empathize with Filipino students.

(24) The present Senators will serve ad-interim as members of the National Assembly, half of then elected in 2016 to serve for six years and those elected in 2013 to serve for three years. Thereafter, half of the National Assembly, one from each Federal State will be elected in 2020, and the other half (one from each Federal State shall be elected in 2023. Members of the House of Representatives shall devolve ad interim as members of the Federated State Assembly, along with all

provincial and the local officials who shall serve until noon of June 30, 2023, and reelected every six years thereafter.

(25) The Philippines shall pursue an independent foreign policy that avoids involvement in the quarrels of strong nations, under treaties that forbid storage of nuclear armaments in our territories, duly concurred in by the National Assembly and, when the National Assembly so requires, ratified by a majority of the votes cast by the people in a national referendum held for that purpose, and recognized as a treaty by the other contracting State.

September 30, 2017

ooooo

END OF BOOK

www.ingramcontent.com/pod-product-compliance
Lightning Source LLC
Chambersburg PA
CBHW051743250726
48659CB00001B/216